Frogs, Cats and Pyramids

Wild Journeys in Search of Knowledge

Frogs, Cats and Pyramids

Wild Journeys in Search of Knowledge

Tony Cleaver

Winchester, UK
Washington, USA

First published by Liberalis Books, 2014
Liberalis Books is an imprint of John Hunt Publishing Ltd., Laurel House, Station Approach,
Alresford, Hants, SO24 9JH, UK
office1@jhpbooks.net
www.johnhuntpublishing.com
www.liberalisbooks.com

For distributor details and how to order please visit the 'Ordering' section on our website.

Text copyright: Tony Cleaver 2013

ISBN: 978 1 78279 410 3

A CIP catalogue record for this book is available from the British Library.

Design: Lee Nash

Printed in the USA by Edwards Brothers Malloy

We operate a distinctive and ethical publishing philosophy in all
areas of our business, from our global network of authors to
production and worldwide distribution.

CONTENTS

Prologue   *vi*

Chapter 1. Mathematics: Shadows: A Hyper-story   1

Chapter 2. English Literature: The Student's Tale   9

Chapter 3. Foreign Languages: The Colony of Frogs   28

Chapter 4. Geography: Road Transport   51

Chapter 5. History: Environmental Impact   80

Chapter 6. Science: A Hitch in Time   92

Chapter 7. Computer Studies: The Millennium Bug   125

Chapter 8. Economics: Across the Wide Star Paths   137

Chapter 9. Faith & Ethics: The Moonlight Cat   144

Prologue

High on the mountain, far from the city, a gathering of conference-goers assembled in a large, wandering, stone and timber residence perched above a spectacular panorama.

They had come from all points of the compass. They were attending a conference devoted to meditation, deliberation and debate. They had come seeking the truth.

Except one.

The place was intended to be inspirational. Introductory speakers had emphasised that the conference offered no ready solutions, no formulas, no key perspectives on how to make sense of a confusing world. It was said that any answers that participants were looking for could only come from within themselves. Hence all had been briefed to attend and bring whatever thoughts, experiences, stories they possessed with them. That was the message: to participate. *Truth could only come from engaging with the intellectual, emotional and spiritual challenges that the gathering hoped to generate.*

The focus for this conference was a rambling series of buildings, which flowed one into another stepping down the mountainside from small dormitories to a central service block, various function rooms, to a larger auditorium. A number of balconies ringed the whole, each cantilevered out over a precipitous, breath-taking view.

During the afternoons, as warm air rose up from the valley bottom far below, clouds would billow and shift about the conference site, causing some to wonder if their elevated detachment from distant humanity was an aid or actually an impediment to their hoped-for enlightenment. Do heads in the cloud help? Does one understand society better for being embraced by it or divorced from it?

Late one cold, clear, star-speckled evening, two men and two women met to converse on a quiet balcony. A slow, chill breeze drifted down from the summits above them. The only noise was a gentle tinkling of some distant mountain stream; that and the sound of thoughts turning over in four very different minds.

"Analysis is the way forward," said Hugo, the scientist. "To examine any puzzle you first have to break it down into its component parts, have a look at each bit and see how it fits together to form the whole. The further you break it down, the closer you get to see how it all operates. Split the atom, examine the nucleus, look into its heart."

"But does that get you any closer to understanding?" asked Ana Maria, the artist and writer. "Might you not be able to see the forest for the trees? Myself, I like to be able to stand back and get the overall picture."

David, a philosopher agreed. "Take your approach to examining a body," he said to the scientist. "You can cut it up, examine all the organs, bones, muscles and fibres, you can figure out how it all fits together and works. But does that get you any closer to understanding what life is? All the component parts are there, like you say. You could even try fitting them back together again, like Frankenstein's monster. But there is some missing spark that is life, or consciousness, that you cannot find. You can flick a switch and pulse electricity all through it but, unlike in fiction, you cannot bring that dead, cold body to wake up. No matter how deeply you analyse it, you cannot unravel the puzzle of what some would call God-given life."

"Shit!" thought Julia, the thief. "I'm out of my depth here. I'd better keep quiet and try and look pensive. Just so long as they don't guess what I'm thinking about."

"But the whole history of science tells us that we can," argued Hugo, getting agitated with the philosopher. "Look at the advances in medicine, for example. People used to explain life and death, conception, births, plagues and disease all as Acts of God. Now we understand so much more. We can artificially inseminate; we can clone life; we can immunise against disease and prevent plagues. Medical analysis has done all that and one day we will certainly understand more about the mystery of the brain and consciousness. There are scientists working away right now, researching these very areas as we speak. The next breakthrough cannot be so far away."

"Your faith in science is no different from another's faith in God," said David.

"There is something irreducibly mystical in all life," said Ana Maria. *"If I aspire to attain truth in art I reach for something that is beyond reason; beyond the rational, analytical mind. It awakens my emotions, it moves me, it resonates with my experience in some way. What is beauty? How can you capture that?"*

Julia jumped. She could say something: "Did you hear they've surveyed a large number of people and asked them to rank a series of photographs of members of the opposite sex according to how attractive or beautiful they find them? I read about that. They found that it is symmetry in the face and body form of others that best explains attractiveness. How about that!"

The other three all laughed.

"OK," said the scientist, *"I accept that that hardly explains beauty in all its forms. I confess that art, especially modern art, is beyond me and my rational mind. I guess art is just a different way of knowing the world than science. In most universities, art schools and places of learning, artists and scientists hardly know how to talk to one another..."*

"Yes — two separate cultures," commented David.

"And yet we have mathematical analyses of art and music — examining the symmetry of what we find pleasing to the eye and ear. We find symmetry throughout nature... we call it harmony... an artistic or musical term which is allied to beauty," mused Ana Maria.

"All quests for knowledge involve a search for patterns," said the philosopher. *"The so-called laws of nature; the movement of the planets; trends, causes and effects in history; the structure of music, composition in paintings... humankind finds patterns everywhere we look. We seek to categorise and fit the world we see according to the abstract constructions we make in our minds."*

"I think I see where you are going..." said Ana Maria.

'I'm glad you can,' thought Julia, as she backed away to look over the balcony, *'just so long as you don't see where I'm going.'*

"Yes," the writer continued, "you're asking are the laws of nature discovered or invented...?"

"The question of whether there is intrinsic Order in the Universe... or only in the mind of the observer is just about the most enduring controversy in humankind's quest for knowledge!" replied David.

"But it really is all connected," continued Hugo. "Pythagoras called mathematics the language of nature. From the earliest thinkers right up to today, the progress of civilisation has been marked by the accumulation of knowledge and its expression in great creations of art and science. From pyramids to cathedrals, from symphonies to space-ships, in all languages and literature, humankind has sought the truth. Truth based on the patient accumulation of all forms of knowledge: maths, language, science, the humanities, art, literature..."

"We ought to invite others to share their thoughts on how they see the world," said Ana Maria. "A historian will have a different point of view to a mathematician or a linguist..."

"And I am continually being reminded that science and technology need to think more about ethics..." said Hugo.

"Well that is why we are gathered together here on this mountaintop – not separated from each other in all our specialisms, in all our different institutions," said the philosopher. "Let us invite whoever wants to join us to come and tell their stories..."

"I agree!" cried Julia, celebrating this turn in the conversation. "Do let's get others to come along and join us. The more the merrier!"

The first one they invited was Ivan, a mathematician. An observant, thoughtful fellow, he had seen the other three in deep conversation as they had walked through one of the function rooms and had enquired what they had been discussing. On being invited to share his thoughts about his own specialism, he was firstly very apologetic.

"Most persons' first reaction to hearing that I study mathematics is horror, then feigned ignorance, then they change the subject!" he said. "I think most people are turned off at school. They think it is too difficult for anyone except boring eggheads..."

"I know how they feel," grimaced Julia.

"*But you don't consider yourself boring, though, do you?*" asked Ana Maria.

"*Of course not. Or rather, I hope not!*"

"*Can mathematics lead to Truth?*" asked David.

"*Listening to you speak, I suppose I would say that it is one way,*" said the mathematician. "*It has the purity of abstraction. Take number – the building block of mathematics. No two items that we can see in the real world are ever identical: one apple is never exactly identical to another apple, for example. But we can abstract from a basket of apples the concept of number – so we can count them: one, two, three, four etc. From there we can conjure up relations, equations and predictions that lead us into purely abstract dimensions... the parameters of other worlds. My story is about that...*"

Chapter I

Mathematics: Shadows: A Hyper-story

Point was pleased with herself.

She was important. She was unique. All around and about her gaped vacant, featureless space and she knew that the only thing that really existed was herself. Wow!

What can you say about nothingness?

Nothing.

Also: *Something* is infinitely better.

Point was something. She had Location. A point in space. When all else is empty and anchorless, was not that something to be pleased about?

Yes.

She breathed confidently. Fixed. Certain. A point of reference and contrast in the surrounding vacuum.

But then… somehow… deep within her… uneasiness moved.

Was there something… missing?

Point could not have had the conceptual framework to describe it, but – in examining the parameters of her entire being – she found the faint Shadow of awareness that dimension was in some way out there. And she did not know what that was.

Dimension? Did it exist? Where? How?

Was she just a pointer to some other reality? A tiny speck in space that hinted at some altogether greater existence?

Point's anxiety slowly grew and grew, but no matter how desperate her search she could not discover any further trace of it in her universe… just the overwhelming frustration of her own limitedness.

She could not be pleased any more.

Line smiled: poor Point. If she could only have looked into

herself a little more penetratingly she would have seen her own thoughts stretching away into that all-important dimension.

Length. Lovely, breathtaking, infinitely-long length.

Whooosh!

Line could go on and on. And when he had finished that he could just as easily come all the way back again. What dimension!

Point could not see it but she herself was that Shadow of one-dimensional Line. How ironic. Line smiled again. He drew himself out of a single dot and soared away in a slim pencil-line to eternity.

And then he stopped.

Self-satisfaction slowly faded.

What if... what if Line was the shadow of something else in turn? Another dimension? Could there be such a reality?

Line tried to conceive of such a thing. Where should he look? Out There somewhere? He raced up to one end: anything further? No. Doubling back he looked out in the other direction. No help there either. Where else? There was not anywhere else! Line dashed up and down again. Zoom. Zoom. All the way to infinity and back again but there was nothing else in his entire world. No matter how hard he looked, length gave no clue to any other dimension.

What a joke! How blinkered can you get? Screaming from one extreme to the other when all he had to do was stop and look around.

Triangle snorted: Huh! She had no patience for stunted intellects like that.

What can you say to uni-dimensional beings who have no concept of Height and Area? How can you begin to explain the immense variety of creations that exist in two-dimensional space? Everything from triangles to polygons; not to mention all those beautiful curves. And yet to unseeing, uncomprehending Line the whole host of wonderful and endlessly-variant two-dimensional shapes all had the same one-dimensional shadow. What mind-crippling ignorance!

Triangle stretched. She pushed out an apex further and further; experimenting with Height. Up, up, and then smugly, narcissistically, she slowly... curved. Was not that wonderful? She lay there now coolly arching round into a crescent. Another twist and her area changed: she metamorphosed into a circle. She went on and on: snaking and twisting and creating: stars, zigzags, loops, ovals, squares and eventually, smilingly, back to being Triangle again. At last she rested.

And then...

It started.

The doubt. The insecurity. The faint suspicion.

Perhaps there *was* something else. Was she the Shadow of something more?

Triangle moved once more: this time searchingly. First the three sides of her own figure. Then beyond – North, South, East and West; so much flat space to move in.

Yet she knew, she knew, that somehow it was hopeless. Whatever it was that was Out There was beyond her...

Joe Pyramid yawned, thrust out an arm and woke up. What a crazy dream!

He decided that he had been working too hard. Studying for maths classes had gone far enough – it was time to rest up a little. It seemed ages now that he had been struggling with this particular assignment and the longer he worked on it the further it appeared to be getting away from him. The last time he had opened his mouth in class everyone had laughed at him.

Joe groaned inwardly and hauled himself up into the day. He resolved not to think about anything for a while.

But it did not work. All the arguments he had got into about light speed and the distant reaches of the universe had really annoyed him and now they would not leave him alone. Over breakfast, all the way through toast and tea, he could not shake his head free from foggy notions of relativity...

If the speed of light was The Limit, then man's ability to reach out into space was destined to be pitiful. A whole lifetime's endeavour could not take you further than seventy or eighty light years distant, Joe surmised. And that was simply nowhere in terms of the staggering distances involved in the universe.

What about all those galaxies out there? Billions of light years distant and racing ever further away while he thought about them. Did it mean we could never reach them; never find out where they were going; never know what was Beyond?

Joe could not accept that. There just had to be a way of breaking out of the confines of this frustratingly three-dimensional existence. There had to be a way of travelling faster than the speed of light.

Damn it all, Joe concluded. At present all we know about the farthest stars is what existed in their space billions of years ago – it has taken all that time for their light to reach us. In the meanwhile, *where are they now?*

Gloomily fumbling over such mental conundrums, Joe was suddenly brought up short. He coughed explosively. Very real three-dimensional toast crumbs were at that moment still trying to decide whether it was Joe's oesophagus or his windpipe that they were supposed to be entering.

A final cough and Joe got up and left the breakfast table. He staggered into the kitchen for a glass of cold water. Sipping and spluttering he found his mind still refused to be distracted by the mere mechanical disorders of its biological support system.

What about another way of looking at things? Stop racing around deep space trying to get someplace: length, height and depth cannot lead anywhere else. Where was the missing dimension?

Shadows. Everything in the universe that can be perceived is simply the shadow of some extra-dimensional reality. How to get there: that was the essence of the problem.

It was a paradox of simplicity and impossibility.

A point cannot see itself as the trace of a one-dimensional line. A line cannot see itself as the shadow of some two-dimensional triangle. And a triangle can search all over the flat plane without ever being able to conceive of the pyramid which soars above it. By mathematical definition, each figure is locked into its own dimensional space and cannot get out of it.

So Joe Pyramid could not see the fourth-dimensional projection of his own volume into some form of hyper-creature.

Just whose shadow was he standing in??

But he was close.

He had learned.

The answer was not Out There on the fringes of some galaxy.

Where was the missing dimension, of which Joe's universe was only a faint shadow? Somewhere all around him, all the time?

In Time he would get it...

She was there, of course. She had been there all along. Watching, smiling knowingly at him. Poor Joe Pyramid.

Joe wrote the day off. It was no good. He would be better going back to bed, getting some decent sleep and starting all over again when his head was properly ready for it. He sloped off back to his bedroom, climbed between the covers, turned over and closed his eyes...

His thoughts flew out – unstoppable – to those damned distant galaxies. There they were: charging away from him close to the speed of light. They blinked and twinkled infuriatingly at him in his mind's eye: catch us if you can, they said.

And then...

And then...

He saw!

He was there! He was looking at those stars right now! His thoughts had flown faster than the speed of light. He had broken clean out of his three-dimensional chamber! He had conquered Time. Joe Hyper-pyramid.

What was necessary – he understood – was to unfold his mind and take it out of the confines of his body and its uni-volume world. Turn himself inside out.

It was dead simple, when you knew how.

It could not be done, of course, by charging around in three-dimensional space allegedly 'awake'. How ironic! Joe kept his eyes firmly closed to 'reality' and took that long and troublesome journey inward. And outward.

Time stopped. She welcomed him. All the galaxies of worry in Joe's three-dimensional world ceased racing away from him.

Time gave him just a glimpse of the mind-expanding hyper-realities that had lain hidden, a world away, beyond his blinkered gaze.

But he could not hold it. He found himself slipping back... folding-in on himself... back into his regular 3-D existence... with its stale toast and cold tea.

Time let him go. She knew he belonged there – a Pyramid.

Instead, Time moved on and addressed herself to her own hyper-reality. There was something that was worrying her; she did not want to waste her efforts on the impossibility of liberating her shadow, Joe Pyramid, from its limited confines.

What really bothered her was the suspicion that Some Other Dimension existed just beyond her grasp and she...

could not...

quite...

reach it...

END

"Wow!" said Ana Maria. "I like that. You can see into other dimensions... That is really mind-bending."

"Yes," said Ivan, bashfully. "We can calculate their properties quite easily; we can conceptualise them, though of course we cannot actually see them in our three-dimensional world..."

"But you have given us an insight into your world; you have shown us one direction where mathematics can lead us," said the philosopher. "Thank you for that. Now stay with us while we pursue other subjects, other disciplines, and see where they can take us also."

"Yes – I'd like to know where Art can lead us," said Hugo. "Ana Maria – can you tell us something about that?"

"If you do, please excuse me for a moment while I take this call," said Julia, waving her mobile at the others. There was in fact no call but she was desperate to escape from the deepening conversation.

"Come on Ana Maria – help us out," said the mathematician. "What makes a great work of art or literature, and can fiction communicate Truth?

"Why yes! Art is the response to the creative instinct: an instinct that we all carry within us but which needs to be nurtured. It is the urge to communicate the truth we find all around us and within us. It is our reaction to something or some person that inspires us."

"But what do you think makes a classic, a great work of art or literature?" asked Hugo. "Is it the passage of time? The opinion of experts? Universal appeal? I've puzzled over that for a long time..."

"I used to think it was some unique skill... that only the Shakespeares, Beethovens and Rembrandts possessed," Ana Maria responded, "but of course now we see all sorts of conceptual art – modern art – that conveys only an idea, which I guess is its main claim to be considered as art. It can be shocking, depressing, humorous, whatever."

"And what is great art? I guess it is a matter of opinion," she continued. "What turns me on may be different to what you consider great art. But the passage of time and the judgement of society – critics and others – determines whether any work of art becomes famous or

not. Van Gogh died penniless and ignored but his paintings are world famous and of enormous value today. Artists are very lucky if they are recognised in their own lifetime. Let me tell you a story about that...”

Chapter 2

English Literature: The Student's Tale

It was a slate grey, rain dull day in Durham. Heavy, moisture-laden clouds cloaked the soaring towers of the city's Norman cathedral and muffled the chimes of its massive bells as they tolled the hour.

The bowed figure of Professor James Allsop, learned authority on medieval English literature, hurried along, trying to pick his way between numerous serpentine rivulets that were coursing down the cobbled streets en route to the river. He had much on his mind.

It was not just that undergraduate student numbers were growing each year faster than the number of staff appointments, or even that postgraduate students seemed to need more teaching these days; but that on top of all this, the demands of administration, of manning committees, of writing reports and monitoring performance in all activities seemed increasingly time-consuming. As a result, quality research time for the English department seemed to be getting squeezed out. Yet it was on his department's research reputation that everything depended: if they scored below what was expected in the next assessment they would lose income, thus staff and thereby future research capacity. How could this vicious circle be squared?

If only his postgraduate students were a more inspiring company! This year's lot seemed a pretty insipid bunch and the applications for next year were a joke. He had only last week thrown an application in the bin – a quick glance had shown it to consist of inarticulate gibberish. Maybe the applicant had thought that inconsistent spelling and grammar were de rigueur in medieval studies? Where oh where was he going to find and

9

publish the paper that would make the world sit up and take note of his department?

Professor Allsop paused to allow a car go splashing by, then he crossed wearily to climb the steep, narrow roadway that led up to the damp, ochre walls of Durham Castle. There were no immediate answers to the problems he mused over. For the time being he had to put these thoughts out of his mind. A glance at his watch showed him he still had fifteen minutes to make it to the formal meal at University College.

Allsop sat three-quarters of the way along High Table and cast a disapproving eye over the numbers of undergraduates eating below him.

"Too noisy!" he grumbled to his neighbour. "Every term they get more boisterous. The Master ought to do something about it."

"Come, come, James," replied Dr Geoffrey Clark, senior lecturer in Law. "They've just got back from their Christmas vacation and no doubt they all have a lot to talk about."

"Yes, maybe you're right," sighed Allsop. "Forgive me but I'm all out of sorts at present. It's this damn research assessment that's got me wound up. I wonder how other departments cope with it."

"Much as we all do, I suppose," nodded Clark in sympathy. "A lot of worrying, soul-searching and scrabbling around to catch the best people. It is not easy for any of us these days, though I must say Physics seem to be very smug of late. They've somehow managed to get it all taped."

"Oh? What's their secret?"

"Blowed if I know, actually. It's all the talk up at Grey College, however. One of our secretaries is married to a research assistant on the Science site and he lunches at Grey. The whisper coming back is they're on to a real breakthrough."

"Humph!! Don't tell me they've been given a load of government money to build atom smashers or something…"

"No, it's not that. I don't think they've won any great research grant as yet. I've got the impression they've found a way to recruit new researchers that is absolutely unique."

"Well they're doing better than I can, if that is the case. I seem to get nothing but dullards or hopeless romantics. I don't suppose it would do any good to ask them – Physics are such an impenetrable lot – but I wonder if they've got any useful ideas for the rest of us?"

"Well you might go up to Grey and ask. Certainly going to the Physics department will be a waste of time – they're all on a different planet there – but a number of them come down to Earth long enough to eat at Grey, by all accounts. Give Vincent a ring and work yourself an invite to their next formal."

"Mmmm. Thanks for the tip. If I get a break from all these students one day, I'll get round to it..." Professor James Allsop turned his attention back to his meal.

The ambitious notion of trying to communicate with physicists was forgotten for the time being as the English department buzzed with the activity of a new academic term. What with lectures, tutorials, meetings and running around in adminis- trative circles, Professor Allsop might have entirely forgotten his conversation at Castle – if it had not been for a smart brown envelope that appeared unannounced in his in-tray one morning. Slicing open the envelope it revealed an invitation to attend a private viewing of an art exhibition at Grey College. The date set was in February – two weeks away on a Thursday evening, and it was to include a formal meal. He decided to call the college to investigate.

"Hello, Vincent, this is James Allsop – English."

"Oh yes, James. What can I do for you?" Vincent Wyatt, the Master of Grey College, had met him a number of times.

"I've just received your invitation to the art exhibition, old boy. Many thanks and all that. I thought I might come along."

"Fine, fine. You'd be very welcome. There have been quite a number already confirmed so I'll add your name to the list. We're arranging this private viewing – mostly Scottish landscapes, y'know – before they all go down to art galleries in London. I hope you'll enjoy the occasion."

"I hope so too – it's a little while since I've been to Grey so it's time I renewed acquaintances... I say, Vincent..." Allsop hesitated a little, "you don't know if you've got many from Physics turning up, by any chance?"

"Well, no, it's not normally their thing, you understand. Apart from a couple of resident postgrads who'll you'll meet at dinner we've got none that I know of attending the viewing... Any reason you ask?"

"No, no, not really. It's just that a couple of chaps were recommended to me. I really must meet them some time."

"Yes, yes, of course. Well, I'll be pleased to introduce you to our residents and any more that might come on the day. All sorts of people will be turning up, I can assure you of that. So: Thursday week... I look forward to seeing you then, OK?"

Allsop thanked his host and hung up. He did not think it would come to anything but 19th century Scottish landscapes were as good an excuse as any to dine at Grey's and widen his social circle.

Grey College stands high on the southern flank of Durham, facing the medieval heart of the city like an old coaching inn on the London Road. As Professor Allsop climbed the hill from the river, the college rose up before him, its central house silhouetted against the evening sky, dark and mysterious, the distant floodlit cathedral reflected eerily in its tall, curtained windows. The wind howled. The clouds above swirled and fought each other and tore themselves into rags. Cold, clinging mists seemed to sweep across the hillside, spilling around the student residences – each an isolated hulk anchored alone in the failing light.

The main entrance hall of the college was huge, silent and empty. Shadows flickered coldly in the low light and a door creaked in the icy breeze that filtered through the building. This cannot be right! Allsop wondered where he should be. Hearing a murmur of noise, he reached a door back and looked down a long, dark, funeral corridor to a pool of brightness and activity at the other end. That looked more like it. Still cold, he gathered his coat about him and strode purposefully towards the light, his footsteps echoing as he went.

As Allsop moved along, the buzz of interaction ahead pulling him in like a bee to a hive, he found himself hurrying to get out of this dark, sombre passageway. The pool of light grew bigger and bigger but – wait a minute – this did not look like a reception for visitors to an art gallery. The noise grew and he began to hear laughter and shouting and the jangled chords of unrecognisable music.

Suddenly a scrum of bodies came bowling out of a doorway on his left and spilled all over him. He bounced into the opposite wall, fending off a sprawling figure as he tried to regain his balance. The heady smell of beer filled the corridor.

"Ooof!... Sorry... gerroff!" A dishevelled young man, his hair slightly better groomed than a haystack, tried to disentangle himself from the melee and make amends to this newcomer he had so rudely ambushed.

"Really... Ha! Ha! Ha!... Very bad show... Oh leave me alone, you animals!" The student dusted himself down, pulled his jacket straight and made an effort to distance himself from the two other buffalos who, grinning and pushing each other, hurried back into the Junior Common Room bar.

"Do you make a habit of crashing out here and rugby tackling anyone passing by?" Allsop enquired acidly. He was not a big man and this assault had shaken his poise and authority.

"Ah! Only if it's a cold night and I need a little exercise to warm me up..." the student replied with a glitter in his eye. "We don't get too many new faces round here so they are fair game..."

Professor Allsop drew himself up in response to this threat and cleared his throat: "Harruumph! I am looking for the art exhibition in this College. I seem to have lost my way..." He was anxious to restore some dignity to the occasion

The student took his arm and steered him further down the corridor. "Wrong building, my dear sir. Let me show you the way, it's the least I can do..." He fixed his companion with a beery grin, his eyes still twinkling amusedly.

James Allsop was distinctly uncomfortable at having a large student – apparently as sensitive as a rhinoceros at a tea party – drag him off into the night but, despite his protests, he lost control of the situation. He found himself thrust out into the dark and cold again, his companion keeping up a stream of chatter.

"I know an artist – brilliant fellow – paints all storms and skies. Talked to him only last week, but he won't come to anything like this. Too shy of the public, you see.

"Well it's understandable, I brought him up here out of his normal surroundings and it shook him rigid. Nervous types, artists – Whoa! Mind that step. Bit of an obstacle course coming up here in the night!"

Allsop almost fell up the pathway rising out of the mist in front of him. He just managed to prevent himself from cursing out loud.

"William Turner, d'you know his work? Done a fair bit 'round here you know. Well of course his early stuff was pretty conventional but when I showed him what some of those Impressionists had done he got really excited. Started experimenting with light, wind, rain and all sorts of atmospherics. Painted castles in the air... Ha! Ha! Ha! Well – here we are. The art exhibition should be in here somewhere..."

They had crossed a damp swathe of grass to arrive at a large, oaken door in the next building. Through a small, opaque square of glass set at head height a number of figures could be seen moving about inside. The student seized the door handle.

"Bugger! It's locked! 'Fraid we've come to this building from the wrong side so there's nothing for it but to traipse round to the front and go in the main entrance. OK?"

Allsop was once more propelled out into the night. Now thoroughly disorientated, he was adrift like a rudderless ship with a crazed captain at the helm. What was this madman talking about? Where was he taking him now?

The older professor and his self-appointed guide stumbled around the back of a long, four-storey building that marked the eastern limit of the college grounds as it fetched up against the wooded hillside. There was a very dark tunnel here between the brickwork on one side and the overhanging trees on the other. Allsop was steered relentlessly into this black hole.

"Yep, I've met some interesting people here in Durham – all down to my work in inter-temporal energy exchange. Physics, that is. What department are you in?"

Professor Allsop was now in almost total darkness in unknown surroundings, being talked to by a complete stranger who he could not see. Even his own voice, coming back to him strained and disembodied in the gloom, seemed unrecognisably foreign:

"Ah... English... down by the riverside..."

"Oh yes. I've only met a few in that field. Shakespeare, of course. And Chaucer – he's a great character. Bundle of laughs. Now there's a man I could take into the bar... if only they didn't keep throwing me out of it... ha, ha, ha! Mind you, how do you manage the language? Bit difficult, eh? Last time I went out with him I told people he came from this remote part of Norway. Dead easy. We all got by with body language and a lot of laughs. Yeah, Geoffrey Chaucer... love's our beer, did you know that?"

Who was this drunken maniac by his side? Still fumbling along in the blackness, Professor Allsop could not believe what was happening. Is this character trying to lecture me on my own subject? Am I not one of the world's experts on Chaucer? Am I? Where am I? Maybe these were all disjointed episodes from some hallucinatory nightmare? He tried to reassert his grip on reality:

"My dear fellow, what do you mean? Are you insinuating that Chaucer was some kind of beer-swilling student like yourself? This seems to be a case of transference ad absurdum…"

His companion came to an abrupt halt and, tightening his grip on his arm, forced Allsop to stop also. The haystack-topped head came looming round in the dark – evidently glaring at the slighter man.

"Are you trying to be funny? Think I don't know what I'm talking about? I've spent years on my research and I know these people, I can tell you…"

Allsop's head began to spin. This was not happening. He wasn't here at all. Here was one of the country's experts on medieval English who had spent some thirty years publishing authoritative works on Chaucer being confronted by a physics student who was telling him he knew more about England's greatest medieval poet than he did. Worse, he was beginning to believe it!

Allsop nervously rallied: "Ahem! I mean no offence… You have me at a disadvantage since I do not know who you are, but I assure you I know Chaucer's work better than almost anyone… I am the professor of medieval English literature in this university. You are not an English scholar are you? Doing research in Physics? Who are you?"

His determined companion, still holding him fast both by a tight hand and a piercing eye, ignored the question and launched into another soliloquy: "I don't mean his works! I don't know his works! I haven't got the time nor the inclination to read what he's written. I mean the man. I know the man! What he looks like, what he sounds like, what he smells like – farts an' all!! Do you know that, Mr Professor? I bet you don't. I bet you know bugger all about the man – whether he's good company or not, what he drinks, which women he fancies... whatever. Actually, he fancies Claudia Morales – third year blonde in Modern Languages... Her room's just above us now, but you can't see it cos the light's out. Bet old Geoffrey'd like to be in there! Ha! Ha! Ha!"

The walking haystack lurched off again, grinning to himself now and hauling his poor, bemused partner after him.

"Come on! We can't stop here in the dark! Too bloody cold!"

The two men reached the end of the long, dark pathway and rounded the corner of the building to a grassy bank, thankfully illuminated by a light above a doorway. The younger man stopped again, his face cracked by an alcoholic leer:

"Look! You haven't got a clue what I'm talking about. Admit it! I'm right, aren't I? Not surprising when half my department don't know and the other half are paranoid about keeping it all hushed up. I'll let you into my little secret, shall I? D'y'know how I know all these people? How I've met 'em? Inter-temporal energy exchange, that's how. I programme my computer to go search for 'em, then I pull them in here. Bit of a shock at first it is, though some come round faster than others. I tell 'em: look – it's all to do with energy. You can't destroy it; it never disappears; it just converts from one form to another. Rearrange the molecules from one space and time to another. A straight swap – easy as that. Actually they don't need to understand it – any more than I know how ducks lay eggs. Old da Vinci cottoned-on quicker than any. Clever bugger, he is. That's what made the penny drop – should've realised earlier – what a way to push back the frontiers, eh? Converse with the best brains in history! Tremendous! C'mon, I'll show you..."

Ignoring Allsop's feeble protestations, the student held open the door behind him and indicated that they should both enter. It offered light, warmth and a refuge from the night.

"Come on... the art exhibition is in here!" he said with impatience.

The younger man led the way down a corridor, keeping up

his nonstop commentary all the time. Allsop by now had given up all autonomy and dutifully followed, as if in a dream.

"See these? All student rooms," he waved an arm at a couple of doors with posters and odd drawings and notices pinned on them, "bloody obvious with all this junk, but we gotta go this way to the conference rooms below."

They reached a stairway and descended one flight. "Look, see that picture there? Gimme a second and I'll show you an art exhibition!"

At the bottom of the stairwell was a large, framed print of Durham Castle and Cathedral, hanging on the wall opposite. The student paused in front of it and delved deep into his jacket pocket. He fished out what looked like a cross between a portable telephone and mini-computer, flipped open a panel and started pressing buttons. Holding the gadget up close to the picture frame he turned his head and grinned at Allsop.

"Now watch this!" he said.

The gadget beeped. Allsop's eyes nearly jerked out of his head. The picture in front of him seemed first of all to glow in brilliant colour, then it flashed on and off several times, as if caught in some strobe light. Then it vanished.

"Huh!!?" Allsop goggled, disbelievingly.

"Take a look behind you," his companion directed.

He did not want to. Professor James Allsop, distinguished member of the English faculty and a recognised authority to whom many deferred in this university, had been reduced to a mumbling wreck too frightened to take a step back and glance over his shoulder. But he had to. The command was irresistible.

"Augh!" Allsop jumped in spite of himself. The picture of Durham was lying at the foot of the stairs behind him.

"Ha! Ha! Ha! Like I said: bit of a shock the first time it happens, isn't it?" The student chortled insanely. "Now d'y'believe me? O'course, this is just a simple move in space but in principle shifting matter through time isn't much different. Once

I'd moved a bit of furniture around like this I got to work on the inter-temporal exchange. With that perfected, I played around for ages but you've gotta ask yourself – what's it all for? How can I use it? That's where da Vinci comes in…"

Allsop was not listening. He walked slowly, gingerly, up to the large picture where it lay, propped up against the wall at the foot of the stairs. He half expected it to jump up and bite him. But it looked perfectly normal – large and heavy, with no strings or anything else attached to it. How on Earth had he done it??

"Watch out!" the other called.

Another beep sounded behind him and Allsop's incredulous eyes watched the picture glow again with golden light, flash once or twice and – zip! – it seemed to jump back on to the wall, resuming its original position.

"Good… good grief!" his mouth dropped open. "This… this is amazing."

"No, not really. Pretty small beer, actually. You soon get fed up playing around like this. Moving people through time is much more of a challenge."

"So… you really have met people… from the past?" Allsop was reluctant to say it out loud as if it were lending credulity to the absurd.

"Lots of times. Yeah: quite natural, when you come to think of it. You're accustomed to run seminars and conferences with visiting speakers who've come great distances across the globe, aren't you? Why not across time?"

"Why not indeed," repeated Allsop vacantly. He was ready to believe anything now.

"The payoff has been tremendous, on both sides. Well… ha! ha! ha! most of the time. Lemme show you: let's go back up to the third floor."

The student turned to the staircase and started climbing enthusiastically, two steps at a time. The somnambulist followed a little more slowly, deliberately. In a couple of minutes they reached the top floor of the building and then turned left, through double doors, to another corridor of what seemed like student rooms. The younger man stopped at the end of the passage, in front of the last door on the right. The name Henry Bright was scrawled on a square card pinned at head height in the centre of the door. Just beneath it, in bold red capitals, it stated: *Radioactive! Danger! Do Not Enter.*

"Welcome, my dear sir, to my humble abode!" Henry Bright flourished an arm and bowed low. He then produced a key, opened the door and ushered his older companion into the interior.

The room was quite large – about 15ft by 20ft – painted dull red with a large window opposite and it was tidier than a scrap-metal yard. A computer seemed to be struggling to breathe beneath a pile of documents on the desk below the window. Clothing was strewn all over a bed and most of the floor. Two worn armchairs faced each other in front of the desk and Allsop was directed to sit in one of them.

"Like a coffee?" No answer to this question was expected. "Have a look at some of these drawings while I make it." Bright pulled out a sheaf of papers from under a pile on his desk and threw them on the other's lap.

Professor Allsop sat dumbstruck once again with a collection of fascinating sketches spilled out in front of him. They were all made in pencil and crayon and depicted various items such as pieces of a telephone, the components of a radio, a series of drawings of aircraft and automobiles. Apart from a number of quick attempts to capture birds in flight, the majority seemed concerned with labelling how things worked. But what language was this? Not Latin? They all looked somehow familiar – had he not seen works like this before?

"Recognise the style?" Bright asked, whilst bent over a hand basin and washing up some coffee mugs. "I said I'd give you an art exhibition, didn't I? Old Leonardo spent a couple of days doodling with those. He was full of questions, too. Wouldn't let me rest much while he was here. Desperate to learn, he was."

"These are the work of Leonardo da Vinci?" Allsop was beyond amazement – he was now convinced that anything his companion told him must be true. He handled the drawings carefully as if they tingled with electricity. "They must be worth a fortune..."

"No they can't be. Da Vinci's portrayals of a telephone? Of car parts? You'd be laughed out of the auction rooms! He can't take 'em back with him either. I wouldn't let him. No. But he goes back with the ideas, you see. He goes back knowing men can fly. That makes all the difference. Before he was just another Italian artist. Now he becomes an engineer, inventor, a genius ahead of his time... geddit?"

"You've done that? You have given him those ideas...?"

"Well how else was he going to invent a helicopter centuries before they were ever built? Someone had to show him, he could never have seen them for himself, could he?"

"But... but that's fantastic... you are changing the shape of history!"

"Well no, not actually. We're just confirming it. The history is already made, but all those inspired advances by men of genius... well they're easier to understand now, aren't they? Mind you, I haven't done much yet. There's plenty of work left to do an' I'm racing to do it before others beat me to it..."

"There are others who are doing this as well??"

"Stands to reason, doesn't it? If I can perfect the mechanism I'm sure that there must be other researchers elsewhere on the brink of achieving the same, if they haven't done it already. Of course, getting anyone to admit to it is impossible... 'specially seeing how it is we have benefited."

"We? What do you mean?"

A kettle boiled and Bright splashed water into two mugs of instant coffee.

"Well the Physics department has benefitted, hasn't it? Call it cross-fertilisation. You wouldn't believe some of the ideas coming out of this. Einstein alone threw out enough research questions to keep the department busy for a generation and there are many more around like him. The really good brains work well in whatever century they're placed. It's fascinating to see it, I can tell you."

"So that's it!" Allsop mused, balancing a mug of coffee amongst the papers beside him. "I wondered what it was you people were on to."

"Yeah… one or two people in Physics want to keep everything jealously guarded within the department… but I can't go along with that. You can't keep knowledge in a straitjacket. Besides which, talking to people like Chaucer, da Vinci… it makes you see things differently. Individual subjects are a modern invention; the really great minds didn't limit themselves in that way. Art, science, literature, ethics – they're all part of the same whole. All variations on a single theme: life… the big picture…" Henry Bright sipped his coffee soberly and pondered. "Least ways, that's how I see it. I'm not interested in promoting the Physics research assessment any more – it's all a bloody numbers game." His face contorted and his voice went into falsetto, as if mimicking some overzealous child counting jellybeans: "Has our department got more points than yours? Has it?... Pah! Who cares!!"

"Umm… yes… of course. Quite right, I'm sure. So… you have been contacting people outside of Physics, then. Chaucer, for example?" Allsop's eyes glinted. He tried to keep his voice calm and his expression inscrutable, but his interest had been aroused. It had been a long time since he had received anything like the acclaim that he felt he was due but now he could see his way to becoming internationally renowned. His own work and the research assessment of the English department could have something monumental to gain here.

Bright rose from his armchair and began to pace the room. "The system's all wrong, don't you understand? Who dreamt up this idea that you can measure advances in knowledge? It's driving us all into a rat race: chasing round all sorts of obstacles, over hoops that some idiot administrators have designed – all for what purpose? The prize is some number given out by a government committee that has lost sight of the greater goal of meaningful knowledge. There's hordes of rats, busying about, researching ever-greater refinements into areas that are of no real use to anyone – all chasing a magic number. Who is seriously gonna read all that junk? What does it all add up to? Jelly beans, that's all! You try explaining that to Isaac Newton or Geoffrey Chaucer. No wonder we went out and got drunk!"

"Yes, yes... please calm down, my dear fellow." It was Allsop's turn to get a little impatient. "No doubt that some university research does look a little obscure at times... but tell me, could you introduce me to some of these fine people you bring through time? Like Chaucer? What do you say, eh?"

Bright ignored the enquiry. "What's it all for? Why have I spent years perfecting this technique? So I can get my department and my supervisor to win first place in some crazy institutional race designed by bureaucrats? No way! We are pushing back the frontiers of knowledge... stimulating debate through the centuries... making great art and science..."

"Ahem!... On the theme of great art..." Allsop was trying to pin down his man, "I would like the opportunity to converse with..."

"Great art! Yes! What is great art?" Bright cut him short. "What makes a classic work of literature? You may think this is bread and butter to you, Professor. Hah! I can tell you that talking to the likes of old Geoffrey makes you see things differently – not that you would know or care."

"What do you mean? I imagine it would be fascinating. I wonder if you could arrange a meeting for me..."

Henry Bright seemed at last to be listening. He stopped pacing the room and tripped over a pair of jeans to come and stare at his companion. The knuckles on his hand gripping the mug of coffee were white.

"Don't tell me you want to meet Chaucer… not you?"

"Well of course, my dear fellow. That is precisely what I would want to do. I have spent years studying his works, haven't I told you all this?" Allsop was getting exasperated. "If he meets anyone in this university, why – it must be me!"

Bright's reaction was totally unexpected. He exploded with laughter. He staggered back, leaned against the door and creased up – slopping coffee from his mug on to the carpet. His face went through several transformations before he could control his expression and return to discernible speech again.

"No, no, no… this is too rich… ha, ha, ha! And don't tell me you'd like to read some of his works as well, something original, like da Vinci's drawings?" Bright seemed to be holding his breath, waiting for the other's reaction and desperately trying not to explode again.

"That would indeed be… interesting…" Allsop would secretly kill for such an opportunity but he was intimidated by the younger man's inexplicable behaviour.

"Haaa!" Bright let out a whoop. "Ho, ho, ho… this really is the limit!" He shook his mop of hair and reached for the door handle. Opening up, he spun outside, trying to get more air to breathe. He held his sides and laughed loud and hard and long as if to shake all the doors off the passageway outside.

Professor Allsop was really irritated by this man's philistine reactions. He rose haughtily from his seat and went out after his host, following a trail of spilled coffee. If it were not for the fact that this research student held the key to the further progression of his distinguished reputation he would have stalked off, leaving this clown to his semi-drunken paroxysms.

"Pull yourself together, young man. Whatever has got hold of you? Straighten up now and stop this ridiculous behaviour!" Allsop was anxious not to let this unique possibility of a personal encounter with the source of his future fame and fortune slip away in someone else's drunken extravagance.

Bright propped his rear against the wall, stiffened his arms against his legs with hands gripping just above the knees, and he raised his head. His face glowed with stifled amusement.

"You're not going to meet Chaucer now... not now you've blown it! You're the last person he would want to meet." He started laughing again.

"Whatever are you talking about? Tell me, what's so damned funny?" Allsop's temper began to fray, sensing he was losing his goal.

"This is really ironic... you should appreciate that of all people, Professor... Don't you understand? You've already read Chaucer's last and most original piece of work! You didn't like it!"

"Whatever do you mean? How can you know what I have or haven't read in my work? This is preposterous!" Allsop began to panic.

"Ha, ha, ha! Listen – Old Geoffrey was amazed when he came here and I told him how famous he was. He told me he wrote *The Canterbury Tales* just to keep his kids happy and couldn't believe it had been hailed over the centuries as one of the all-time classics of English literature. When it sunk in, he got quite enthused about it. Said he'd write another tale as a present to this century, this university. Sort of: thanks for all the fame and that."

"What...? Another chapter to *The Canterbury Tales*...? Where... show me... what happened to it?" Allsop gulped.

"You dummy! Don't you know? I sent it to you! One of the postgrads in your department got word back to me to say that you'd rejected it. Thrown it out! 'Inarticulate gibberish' you were quoted as saying..."

"What!" Allsop's head reeled. He staggered back. Surely this couldn't be happening.

"Don't you remember, old chap? 'A Traveller's Tale' he called it, I think. Even tried to translate it into modern English. Made quite an effort. You must recall it: Chaucer's last and most original contribution... *and you ripped it up!*"

Allsop wasn't listening any more. He wandered off down the corridor not knowing where he was going, his mind in a fog. Could this be true? Didn't he recall some barely intelligible scrib-blings that seemed to parody medieval literature? What he thought was someone's pretentious attempt to imitate Chaucer and curry favour with himself? Surely not that essay he had torn to shreds in one angry postgraduate session? Not that one...

But with every step, his heart sank even further. Yes. It was true. He had read this paper. Professor Allsop descended the stairs as if he was sinking into the depths of some private damnation. The blackness of the cold night welcomed him once more as he stumbled out of the last door. Oh cruel fortune! There was something peculiar about that essay he had discarded – written in an inconsistent hand and capturing hallucinatory fragments: images of pilgrims' clothing mixed with speeding motor cars; of medieval rhyme and snippets of modern vocab-ulary. He recognised it all now. Was it modern or ancient liter-ature? Whatever, it had all been shredded over a week ago. Too late, too late. Oh no! No!

"Hello, James, you're looking a bit lost." It was Vincent Wyatt, Master of Grey College, appearing out of the darkness. "The art exhibition is this way, not far to go now. We have some wonderful landscapes this time; real classic works of art that a man of your culture I'm sure will appreciate. Do come and see..."

END

"Ha! Ha! Ha! I like that!" said Ivan. "It certainly rings true to me and the sort of stuffed shirts that I've met in academic circles, not to mention cocktail parties, exhibitions and other social gatherings."

"Yes, not all society is like that, of course, but you do meet a fair share of people, I call 'em culture vultures, that do like to pontificate on what they think is good or bad art," said Ana Maria. "In the end, it is all subjective."

"I'm not so sure," said David. "As you said, time will tell. There is something universal about great art that is more than just personal opinion. It does communicate great truth."

"Only if you understand its language," groaned Hugo. "I have to say I have great difficulty sometimes figuring out what some artists, writers and musicians are trying to communicate."

"Now there's a lead into our next enquiry," said the mathematician. "Why don't we ask a linguist to tell us his or her story?" He suggested they approach some other conference-goers who had been sitting at some distance from them across the balcony.

Whilst the storytellers moved to introduce themselves to the other party close by, the one woman who had left and not reappeared was meanwhile elsewhere, on her own, looking quietly for the residential quarters. She had no interest in returning for some time.

"A tale of language and communication? I'd be glad to talk about that, if you would allow me," said one man who had been with the other small party. He had been drawn into listening, fascinated, to what the writer had been narrating to the others.

"Please join us, all of you," said David, the philosopher, inviting the two groups to come together. "We have a long way to go yet in our communal adventure. We are on a pilgrimage through all the forms of knowledge and the more we have who can contribute, the better."

"Well as someone who has always loved learning different languages," said the newcomer, Abdul, "I've always been fascinated at the different worlds, different cultures, they can lead you into." He began his tale...

Chapter 3

Foreign Languages: The Colony of Frogs

It was a deep, dark, disused well that rested out of sight in a lonely field. It must have provided water once for some purpose but the farm buildings around had long ago fallen into disrepair and the few residents of these parts had moved away, looking for their futures in distant, more prosperous lands.

Time in this country moved slowly on and nature eventually reclaimed the unused paths, the broken brickwork, the planted woodland whose young saplings once grew in some semblance of order.

At the bottom of the well, deep down away in total isolation where nothing had stirred for years and years on end, the miracle of life was also quietly at work: a small colony of big-eyed, pale-coloured frogs grew...

"Ha ha! Gottit! You'll have to jump higher than that if you want to eat as well as I do."

It was the King Frog – bigger, stronger and, naturally enough, better fed than the others around him. Only when he had had his fill and had bagged the tastiest-looking flies that buzzed down here could his smaller kinfolk have their chance.

"It's not fair! Why couldn't you stay over on the other side of the puddle? There are plenty over there and that one was circling down ever closer to me... Oww!"

"You mind your tongue when you're speaking to me." The King Frog trapped the smaller one beneath him and bit him again. "A little more respect is called for unless you want to go without food permanently..."

"OK! OK! Lemme go. I'm sorry, Your Majesty, of course you can eat whatever flies you like. Oww!"

The small frog limped away, cowed, but wiser to the ways of his world.

And so it was in this little colony – like any other. All have their customs, their language, their ways of going about business. Although the King Frog was a strict and fearsome tyrant to those who dared to challenge the social hierarchy, he was in all other respects a fair ruler who guarded his domain and tried to ensure that peace and order reigned.

Generally speaking, the frogs were happy in their world of mud and gloom. Although brightened only by a small disc of light far above them at the top of the well, their eyes had grown large and there were just enough flies zipping around for all to have enough food. So they were a contented group: hopping and bopping about in dimly-lit puddles living the froggy equivalent of the good life, hidden away from the rest of the world.

Then one day the untroubled bliss of this isolated colony was broken forever. It was a sound that did it: a song; a foreign language that floated down to them from on high. No one knew what it was or where it came from at first. It was haunting, melodic. It was pure magic. Only faintly discernible; almost completely unintelligible but it hung and trembled in the thick, heavy air at the bottom of the well and it sang of a different world.

Five or six frogs separated from the rest were the first to hear it. They were mesmerised; bewitched. None of them could move. They looked at each other blankly.

"Wot? Wotzit I hear?" Bounder stammered in wonder and fright.

"Dunno!" blinked Skippy, paralysed.

They began to look around. Nothing looked different. Out in the centre of the puddles the King Frog was feeding, surrounded by the rest of the colony. Splashing and croaking in the gloom they were all busily engaged in the daily competition to leap the highest and catch the most dinner. Loud, brash, aggressive, everything seemed normal enough.

But here at the edge of their world, where the Great Curved Wall soared above them and defined the limit of all that could be known, a shimmering, echoing song came whispering down to its tiny, awestruck audience. It was something so… so wonderful. It was *different*.

The frogs hopped closer to the wall. The sound was easier to catch here. First one, then another put his forelegs up on the towering stonework – as if reaching as high as possible to this mystical language. All fell silent, straining to capture every last syllable of the wondrous music.

"Hey! Wot they doin'?"

It was Slugg, one of the king's lieutenants, who noticed the line of frogs stretched up, each almost vertical on their horizon.

"They've found a feast – and they're keeping very quiet about it. C'mon!" the King Frog ordered.

The whole colony came leaping and splattering over to the wall:

"All right, you fellers – no keeping it all to yerselves. Wot you got?"

"Yeah! Share 'n' share alike…"

"Not saying nuffin' – plain selfish I call it."

A chorus of shouting and croaking burst about the small, silent group of listeners.

"Sssh! Be quiet. Please listen!" Skippy pleaded.

"Er?? *Listen?* Woffor?"

"Where's the food? I can't see anyfing up there!"

"No, there's nuthin' to see. You gotta listen… quick… it's fading… it's going… Aaaah! It's… it's… gone."

A forlorn croak broke from Bounder and he slumped down into the mud. The others of the group all similarly slid down to face a circle of scornful, disbelieving faces.

"Wot you croaking on about? Listen?? Listen to wot? You got some insects flying around you never heard before?"

"No... no... it's not the sound of insects... it woz something totally different... like a... a language I don't understand..."

It sounded so lame when Bounder tried to explain it. Surrounded by blank, uncomprehending faces, he began to doubt it himself.

"It came whispering around us... from where we dunno..."

Skippy tried to help, but she ran out of confidence when she saw the reaction of all the others.

A moment's incredulous silence was followed by a great explosion of jeering and belching from the crowd of newcomers. The King Frog hopped forward and bowled over the smallest of the listeners into the slime:

"Wotta loada toadies! You got mud in your brains or sumfin? Hearing strange noises!! Your ears'll be buzzing alright if you waste any more of our time over here – we'll bang your heads together! C'mon – let's get back to feeding."

With that the colony turned and hopped back into the centre of the well. The small group of frogs that had been separated from the rest reluctantly joined and followed their kinfolk. With the whispering song now inaudible there was nothing left to hold them back.

Days passed with nothing more to break the normal routine. The little group of frogs had not forgotten their magical experience but they returned to the busy contest of catching their food. Whenever they could, however, each one would find themselves hopping over to the Wall in the pretence of searching for flies – but all the time ever alert for the faintest sound of something different, something foreign, fantastic.

One twinkling eye met another:

"Anything??" No further question was necessary; the meaning was instantly understood.

"Nope..." came the sighing response.

Greyslime, an older, sourer, distrustful female in the colony – more observant and altogether more suspicious than most –

noticed the continuing tendency of certain members of the community to keep returning to the Wall. She was determined to see what they were after. Not needing to continuously feed her slower body, she could afford to stay longer at the edges of their world and quietly watch the actions of those she disliked.

But their behaviour was hard to figure out. At first, the quiet whispering of occasional couples suggested that they were up to some kind of plot – though each one actually seemed more interested in wandering alone, silently waiting by the stonework. Waiting for what? None showed any interest in searching for flies.

On her own, the wizened old Greyslime set off by herself to mimic their movements. Exactly what were this strange group looking for? Why was it here by the damp, looming bricks they always waited?

And then, crawling slowly out of one shallow, glinting puddle, she suddenly froze in fear. A faint, high-pitched, alien soliloquy surrounded her. Whispering, directionless and completely foreign, she did not know what it was, where it was from or how to cope with it. A small, frightened croak involuntarily belched forth from her throat.

The bewildered call and the paralysed body language was instantly recognised by certain kinfolk. Within seconds, a couple of frogs had bounded up close. Desperate to hear, senses all aquiver, their attitude was less fearful, more confident and openly impatient to investigate this eerie sound and all that it meant.

The chattering, twittering language rose and fell in waves. Looking around, it seemed almost certain to those listening intently that the sound was coming floating down from above.

"Wotzit? Wotzit I hear?" cried Blurt.

"Wotzit... wotzit?" echoed Lumpy.

More frogs came bounding up. The agitated croaking beckoned an increasing number to stop what they were doing and to come on over and listen. As the strange, musical language continued to float around them it stimulated a barrage of comments from the ever-growing audience.

"There! Din't we say you had to listen?"

"I'nt it wonderful?"

"It's weird... it's alien... I don't like it..."

"It's from the devil!"

"No! It's *heavenly*."

"But wotzit saying?"

The sour old Greyslime had had time to recover from her fright on discovering the sound and with many of the colony all around her she was now strong enough and wily enough to try and regain the initiative:

"Dunno wot it says but, wotever it is, it don't belong here. It sounds like some dangerous foreign nonsense. Cast it out! Close your ears to it, I say. GO 'WAY!"

She raised her voice and croaked her command as loudly as her old lungs would allow.

All this commotion finally summoned the King Frog over to see what was going on. Interrupted again during his feeding time, he came with a lieutenant on either side of him and an angry, impatient expression set across his face. What he found on arrival at the Wall was a chorus of belching and burping frogs in fierce argument over the significance of what they had heard. Such a dispute displeased him even more.

"Quieten down the lot of you. Silence I say! Wot's got into everyone all of a sudden? I've never seen such disorder."

"There's some stupid foreign gobbledegook these frogs have heard an' are goin' crazy about..."

"Who's crazy? Who's stupid? Jus' cos it's sumfin you don't understand..."

"STOP IT AT ONCE!" the king bellowed. "I want no more of this indiscipline. If you don't shuddup straight away I'll flatten your bones into the mud."

Blazing eyes and a large, inflated body moved menacingly forward to silence the quarrel.

All argument ceased. Order in the colony was restored. No one was willing to openly challenge the dominant authority when he was so incensed. With black looks and suppressed mutterings the frogs dispersed. But battle lines had been drawn and, if the source of the dispute had again mysteriously disappeared, the colony was now divided as never before over the meaning and significance of this strange foreign intervention.

Older kinfolk, up until now dutifully respected by their younger brethren and whose advice had always been listened to with attention, now found that their efforts to ridicule the strange language and to stress the importance of settling back into old routines were being ignored. Growing numbers of frogs talked about the new phenomenon in their lives. The fact that some old dodderers could not, would not accede that this alien language had any value only served to increase its attractiveness. Some cocky young bucks took to mimicking its high-pitched chatter and called it out to one another – more often than not just to annoy the stuffier members of the colony. But most important of all, like a slow, barely-noticeable undercurrent swirling away beneath the surface of the community, the fact that something existed outside the grasp of them all and clearly beyond the capacity of their leaders to explain it satisfactorily was fundamentally disturbing.

The King Frog continued to deny that anything had changed. He still had not heard the language and would not tolerate anyone else talking about it. However, this standpoint only increased his growing isolation. His rule continued to be accepted by the young discontents simply because he was bigger and stronger than any of them, but there was no other basis to his authority. A grumbling resentment was growing.

Then one day something absolutely amazing happened. It was the resurgence of the language that heralded it. This time, after days and days of silence, the haunting song burst upon the frogs with an urgent persistency. It swelled in volume and rolled echoing about the walls of the well. Tweeting and chirruping as never before, it was impossible to pass it off this time as something irrelevant, something not worthy of comment, all the product of someone's imagination.

"*Listen* to that! Wow! Din't we always say it was fantastic?"

"Wot izzit? Wotzit all about?"

"It's wailing... crying... It's the sound of the devil!"

"No, no! It's gotta be sumfin good, sumfin great. It's so tuneful."

"Maybe there's some really big insect up there..."

"Wait! Look! Look up there. LOOK! It *is* an insect..."

Lumpy had frozen in excitement and was pointing urgently upward. There far above them, silhouetted against the bright disc that was the roof of their world, a fluttering black dot could just be seen. It flew like no other insect they had ever seen before, however. It seemed to grow bigger and smaller; it changed shape; it flew out of sight and then reappeared and, all the time, it *sang*.

A mad chorus of croaking and belching broke out. For some frogs it was the confirmation of something wonderful that they had been talking about for weeks. For others it was something fearful and frightening that they did not understand and did not want to acknowledge in their world. Feelings ran high and the argument was now furious. The King Frog bellowed loudest of all in the attempt to assert his authority, but no one was listening to anybody. The clamour was deafening.

A mile in the sky, warm in the sun, the skylark's melody died in his throat. Originally inspired by the technicolour panorama that was spread all about him, the skylark had floated on the breeze and sung his heart out. For days he had toured the countryside, celebrating the summer in his own inimitable style. Now his happy song was suddenly drowned by an unearthly, demoniacal squawking. Magnified by the walls of the well as if by some giant megaphone, deep-throated, guttural roars surrounded him.

At first the skylark thought it was the sound of death: the Devil was calling him from Satan's dungeon. His wings stopped beating and he began to slip earthward paralysed with fear. The awful croaking continued and he fell towards it like a stone, gripped by panic and unable to save himself. Then, thankfully, a warm updraught caught his stalled feathers and, turning him slowly, it delayed his descent. The raucous hollering from below grew fainter – its spell was broken.

The skylark recovered the use of his wings and he hung there, hovering on the warm air, his brain racing to explain the dreadful fright he had received. The noise coming up to him was less insistent now and he could thus search for its source without it blotting out all his senses. Keen eyes surveyed the field below – first one side, then the other. At last he spotted it: a deep, black hole far beneath him that he had never noticed before, camouflaged as it was in the shadow of an overgrown hedgerow. The desperate roaring was emanating from this hole; obviously some poor creature had fallen into it and was now crying for help.

The skylark was a kind-hearted soul. He was a creature of the sun and summer breezes who enjoyed the freedom of the skies, and the thought of someone trapped down there in that beastly black hole filled him with absolute horror. Closing his wings tight into his body he came arrowing down to the rescue. Alighting on the broken stonework at the top of the well he carefully peered over into its chill, murky depths.

"Are you alright? Who are you? What have you done?" he called out.

The sound of rescue and help close at hand obviously caused the creature below to redouble its roaring and cries of pain. The skylark was much impressed but, what with the distortion of sound caused by the echoing walls, he could not actually make out what was being said.

"Don't worry! I'll help you. Let me figure something out."

The cries below quietened a little and then broke out louder again. It sounded now, listening closely, as if there were more than one voice involved. Maybe there were *two* creatures trapped down there? It seemed difficult to believe. The skylark looked all about him as if searching for what best to do.

He hopped forwards once more and looked over again, deep into this wound in the earth. A plaintive croaking was now coming up to him. The skylark shuddered. This was not a place he would wish for his worst enemy, but he could not ignore the plight of whoever it was had fallen into this hole. He had to do something.

There was only one thing for it. He knew that somebody had to go down there and assess the situation and he knew also that, apart from himself, there were few who had the ability to attempt such a vertical descent and succeed. With a deep breath he spread his wings, plucked up all his courage and launched himself into the rescue. It was an extremely brave thing to do. Down, down, tunnelling into the cold earth he plummeted until he reached the bottom of the well.

With a rush of air, this messenger from the skies landed suddenly amongst the colony of big-eyed frogs. What a commotion! What cries of astonishment! This was an absolutely astounding, frog-boggling revelation. Was it an angel? An alien? The Coming of the Prophet? Or the Devil? Its eyes shone. Its body throbbed with heat. And then it *spoke*.

A rich, full chirruping flooded the well. The faint, foreign language the frogs had once heard gently floating down to them from on high now reverberated all around. The colony was stunned into awestruck silence.

Skippy, one of the smallest frogs who had been amongst the first to hear this language, recovered the quickest. She took a pace forward and, bowing down with eyes aglow, she greeted this apparition:

"O wondrous creature... Who are you? Where do you come from? Of wot can you tell us?"

A torrent of alien syllables and rolling accents was the reply. It was dazzling.

The interchange served to jerk the King Frog out of his frozen state. This was a threat to his sovereign rule of the world and he was having none of it. He leaped up:

"Get back, demon! You shall not invade this blessed earth! I protect this glorious place and you have no business here. Go! Go back to the Fires of Damnation where you belong!"

It was the commanding croak of authority.

The aggressive cry and posture of this dark, looming creature was enough for the skylark. He was not looking for trouble in a hellhole like this. In an instant he was airborne, flapping rapidly and, with his wings shuttering the light, he rose quickly up, up and away. The frogs saw this amazing flying creature grow smaller and smaller and then, in a blink of a wing, it flew across the white disc above them and vanished.

Things could never be the same after that. They had been visited by a being from Outer Space! It changed *everything*. The frogs' entire concept of themselves, their world and what lay beyond had been shaken to its foundations. And whatever It was had come from Up There!

No one had ever dreamed there was anything above them at the other end of the telescope – nothing alive, and certainly nothing worth singing about. It was just a flat white disc that regularly got darker and lighter again – like a light panel with a dimmer switch that the God Frog turned up and down. Or so it was thought until now.

Furious and open debate could now no longer be contained in the colony. Inevitably, the challenge to the rule of the King Frog was not long in coming. The small Skippy was the driving force. She was a free spirit who saw quicker than most the implications of all that had happened. She urged others to action:

"Don'tya see? There's another world Up There and we can have contact wivvit. It's just the King who's standing in our way. All that crap about how wonderful it is here! It's only wonderful for him. I wanna see that creature again..."

"So wadda we do? Ask the King if we can call out to this other world? He'll go crazy. He'll kill us!" worried Blurt.

"No he won't. He can't if we all hang together. 'Specially so if we get more on our side."

"We ask around, eh? See how many want to know about wots Up There?" grinned Bounder.

"Yeah! Let's do it."

And so the whispering campaign started. It was easy at first – there were many who had been disturbed by what they had all seen and heard and, even for some of the fearful ones, like it or not they had to know more about this creature that had appeared. Slowly, in ones and twos, members of the colony were asked their opinion and were persuaded to back a call to investigate the matter further.

Then they came up against the opposition. Slugg the senior lieutenant intervened: "Waddya talkin' about? There's no other world, you idiots! Some crazy overgrown insect that lives up close to the Great White Disc and you start believing in anything. Shuddup and get back to your feeding or the King'll get to hear of this!"

"That's not good enough! We can't just ignore such strange goin's on and continue behaving as if nuffin's happened. There's sumfin very odd Up There an' I wanna know wot it is!"

The spirited Skippy refused to be put down. In defiance, she sat back on her haunches, lifted her head and called out her loudest:

"COME BACK! Come back, O flying one, and visit us again!"

Her urgent cry echoed round and around the walls of the well. It was an open and direct rejection of the King's authority. It was a call for revolution. It had to be met with instant and extreme retribution or there would be anarchy.

The King Frog wasted no time. He came crashing wildly through dark, glinting puddles and in a second he was upon the young female, biting her savagely. She squealed out pitifully but he only redoubled his assault. Flattening her into the mud beneath him he bellowed out his anger:

"How dare you! Wot disobedience! I have given the order for that demon to go and you're gonna suffer for this."

"Let her be!" A group of worried-looking frogs confronted the King. "Don't hurt her any more. She's not the only one who wants your order changed. We all wanna see that creature again."

"Oh ho! A conspiracy, eh?"

The King turned away from the prostrate form of the small frog beneath him to size up this new situation. Glancing about he saw five nervous but determined young bucks facing him and others hopping up to take positions behind them. At his own back he could count two of his lieutenants and a few older and slower members of the colony in support. Others stayed their distance with heads bowed, not wishing to get involved. Even Bugsy, one of his lieutenants, was looking worried and would not meet his gaze.

The King Frog was no fool. He managed to contain his anger and adopted a concessionary tone of voice to the number in front of him:

"Now wot is all this then? You don't seriously believe that our strange visitor has anything good to bring us? I'm looking after your best interests, my friends. There can be no better life than this."

It did not work. Coughing and spluttering beneath him, a tiny voice croaked forth:

"We don't believe it any more. We gotta see for ourselves wots

Up There."

There were cheers of encouragement. Beaten but not bowed, Skippy crawled painfully out of the slime. Friends came to help her up.

Then an older, cynical voice joined in, dripping with sarcasm: "So wot we gonna do then? Start calling out for Unidentified Flying Objects? Where's that gonna get us?"

"It's no good, Greyslime," Bounder retorted. "We gotta do sumfin. We ain't gonna return to your old ways."

An argument began to get going. Again opinions were shouted out and chaos beckoned as one frog tried to outdo another.

Then a flickering in the light stopped them. A breath of warm air wafted down. Skippy, though bruised and bloodied, gasped as she realised what it meant.

"Ahem!" A high-pitched voice in a strange accent fell to their ears. "Deed I hear zat you wan' help? Izzat so?"

It was the skylark, hovering magically above them.

"See you, I speaka your language... let me come down and to you talk a little, yes?"

In the dumbstruck silence which followed this broadcast the skylark folded his wings and dropped lightly amongst them. Instantly all quarrelling was forgotten; the astonished frogs drew back into a wide circle around their alien visitor. They waited for him to speak again.

"I couldn't rest," the skylark explained in a high treble song. "I kep' thinking of you poor folk trapped down here in zis hole. Awful, yes? So I found some of your bruzzers nearby. I listen' to zem. Got to learn your tongue. Ze dialect is strange for me, but it is ze same Animalspeak, yes? So you wan' to escape, no? I gonna help you, don' worry."

Consternation! This apparition was speaking their own language! True, the frogs did not understand all that it talked about, but: Awful? Escape?? There were a few at least who could identify with that. An agitated whispering started amongst them.

Again it was Skippy who was the first to humbly reply: "O beautiful one, please tell us: Who are you? Where do you come from? Of wot things do you speak?"

"I come from above, of course," their visitor chirped. "Where ze sun shines in ze blue sky. I am a skylark. You mean to say zat you *don't know*?" He was appalled.

For the next few minutes conversation was very difficult as it dawned on both parties the extent of the other's ignorance. The frogs were naturally the most disturbed.

"Is there *really* another world up there?" one fearful voice asked.

"But of course, my friends. Ze blue skies, ze green fields, sparkling rivers and ze warm air zat turns you 'round and around in a dazzle of colour. Ze colours! Ze colours... you gotta see ze colours. Not like down here in zis dark and dismal hole. I gonna help you escape, yes?"

"Enough of this witchcraft! You devil... you Satan... this is the language of lies and trickery. He is leading you to death and destruction. Don't believe a word of it!" Bloated with anger, the King Frog splashed forward, determined to stop this alien's influence.

"NO, NO! Please let him alone! Don't!" A desperate Blurt tried to divert the King's furious charge, but it was no use. For the second time, the skylark could see danger threatening to engulf him and was quick to react. In a blur of wings he flickered in front of his hosts for a split second and then he vanished. It was breathtaking, astounding, frog-stopping stuff, like everything else about this wonderful creature. But he had gone.

The sense of bewilderment and shock was all-engulfing. Everything in the frogs' universe seemed to reel around. They had talked, it seemed, to a creature from Somewhere Else and, although communication had been difficult and they had heard of concepts and ideas that were way beyond their grasp, there was one thing that remained clear above all: there was Another Way. For Skippy and her friends in particular, this had enormous implications. Now they could hardly conceal their resentment of the King Frog any longer. There was a better life out there somewhere and this monstrous dictator was standing in their way of getting to it. Others of the colony were more nervous and less sure of all the skylark represented, but very few now were openly in support of their king. That something existed outside and beyond their limited world was undeniable; it brought into question all that they regarded as normal and for some there was no end to their discontent.

And just what *were* colours?

Up above amongst fields of gold and light, the skylark tried to figure it out. What were these frogs doing there? Obviously the biggest one was terrorising the others and keeping them, literally, in the dark. How had they got trapped down there? There was no way to tell. Were they suffering terribly under their tyrannous regime? It seemed so. Maybe they were being punished for something?? The cries that emanated from the darkness sounded in turns desperate; mournful; in pain. Those poor prisoners! They had been denied access to sunlight, warm earth, flowing streams and all the myriad experiences of the wide country. And what company did they keep? Had they ever talked to their brothers of the riverbeds, their neighbours of the fields and skies? Did they *know* what birds were? or fish? or humanfolk? The innocent, awestruck manner with which the little frogs had addressed him moved the skylark profoundly and the contrast with the dark, looming aggression of the King Frog could not have been greater. Clearly the frogs had to be liberated from their living hell. Any sun-loving creature of the open air would have thought the same. It was the skylark's obvious duty to help the poor, oppressed little frogs to overthrow their evil tyrant and escape into the light.

But how was this to be done without risking any further confrontations with the Big Frog? That was not an easy question to answer. It taxed the skylark's mind awfully and would not let him rest. He had to do something more subtle, more clandestine, yet at the same time demonstrably effective…

Little frogs, little hostages: you were not forgotten!

"We've gotta do it!" Bounder was insistent. "You know we have to. We just can't go on sitting here for the rest of our lives wondering what's Up There. We gotta know!"

"But it'll be one hell of a fight – the King'll go crazy, and who knows what others will join him?" Lumpy protested.

"But that's down to us," Skippy explained. "If we prepare our ground thoroughly there'll only be a few who'll support him. So we must isolate him first of all – goodness knows it shouldn't be too difficult. He's such a brute!"

As if to confirm these words there came an explosion of roars and curses from the centre of the well where the King Frog was feeding with his lieutenants. The small band of the friends, as usual grouped together near to the Great Curved Wall, saw a lot of agitated movement and a great deal of spitting coming from their leader. One of the frogs close to him seemed to be croaking in disagreement as he backed away. Then the King leaped forward, there was a sudden riot of mud and water, and the other frog disappeared from view for a few seconds. When the argument was over, the King remained alone in the centre of the well and his adversary could be seen hopping slowly away: mud-spattered, breathing hard and obviously now out of favour. It was Bugsy, the ex-lieutenant.

Skippy wasted no time. She quickly made her way round to where Bugsy had reached the company of some friends. Careful not to overplay her hand, she simply waited to hear what had happened.

A sullen, smouldering Bugsy was complaining in a low voice:

"I simply asked him wot did he make of it – this strange flying fing speaking to us. Wot did he reckon woz Up There?"

"That's all? An' he lost his temper?"

"Yeah! Crazy toad!" Bugsy rubbed a sore shoulder.

"It's cos he's got no answer." Skippy quietly intervened. "But thanks for asking, anyway. We all want to know..."

Others nodded in agreement. Yes: they wanted to know. *Everyone* did.

Skippy was right. The colony was in crisis and the King's wild tirades were no solution. It became obvious to even the most reluctant that their leader was losing all popular consent to his rule of their community. As time passed, the King took to touring continuously around his fiefdom, growling fiercely at any group of frogs that were not busy feeding, at any that aroused his faintest suspicions. He trusted no one, nor had he any response to their worries or concerns except further aggression and the resort to sheer force to keep order. It could not last. It only needed a push now for the whole frog hierarchy to come tumbling down.

Then quickly, quietly, miraculously, the skylark reappeared. He dropped swiftly into the gloom and came to land at the bottom of the well near some small frogs gathered on the edge of the puddles.

"You wan' escape, yes?" he whispered, crouching low to escape attention. "Ze Big One, he keeps you prisoner, yes? You gotta go against him. Why you always let him do what he wants?"

The tiny, frightened frogs looked with big eyes at their visitor. They were captivated.

"You gotta get free," urged the skylark, "don' you see? Come up to ze colours, breathe ze fresh air..."

Other frogs had now noticed the alien newcomer and were coming round to listen to him: pale, cold, innocent and ignorant they were drawn to him like insects to the light. The skylark almost cried – how could he explain it all? They knew so little: if only he could make them *see*…

He tried his best. But how could he describe the infinite expanse that lay outside to creatures who had no concept, no language for anything much beyond their own noses? Struggling in their ugly dialect, he tried to sing songs of green pastures, of rolling meadows, of trees that scraped the sky: strange alien pictures of which the frogs had no knowledge. "Ze space… ze light… ze freedom. You gotta see… Don' let ze Big Frog stand in your way!"

The skylark stopped. As more and more frogs began moving in his direction he could not risk staying any longer. "OK… OK! I go now, my friends, but I come back soon… *What you gonna do meantime?*"

It was a very pointed question. In a rush of air, their visitor from Up There disappeared once more, but the question he left behind hung there, floating in their minds between them all.

Well if they did not understand anything about trees or meadows, or what green was, they all certainly understood the bird's revolutionary talk. In the silent, heavy air the full meaning of all that they had seen and heard over the last few, unsettling days began to grow upon them. No one uttered a sound. The sombre weight of what had to be decided transfixed them all. Minutes ticked by.

"Well then? We *know* wot we gotta do, don't we?" It was Bounder who broke the silence.

"There's no other way," Skippy sighed. "We've talked all about and around it and we keep on coming up with the same answer. It's all or nothing."

"No more talk. Let's do it!" A voice broke out from the back of the group. It was grim, resigned, determined. It was Bugsy.

It took a lot of courage. It needed a lot of tiny frogs to do it. But with steadfast and resolute leaders, with reason, right-eousness and a sense of destiny on their side they got up enough strength and support to do it. With scarcely a signal between them, they all turned and made their way towards the centre of the well. Slowly, one by one, the number of frogs about and behind the King Frog grew in number. Bad tempered and preoccupied with keeping others out of his way so he could continue feeding, he never saw it coming. Bugsy, Bounder and Lumpy got closer; Skippy urged others to follow, and then... they JUMPED!

It was a fearful struggle. The King Frog was big and strong and he lashed out fiercely on all sides, but his attackers were undaunted and there were too many of them. The blows kept coming; he tried to keep his head above it all but slowly, slowly he was forced down. The darkness closed in upon him. Finally... he croaked his last.

The assailants drew back, some breathing hard. Others of the colony crowded around and they all looked at the broken form of their king, spread-eagled before them. It was done. There was no turning back now. The end of an era was signalled by that large, unmoving, unrecognisable shape slumped in the centre of the puddles.

In the sombre, awesome silence that followed, no frog could move. One started to sniffle. Others began to doubt the wisdom of what they had just done. A dull, grey mood settled amongst them. And then in the heavy gloom once more they heard the distant rustle of feathers and felt a faint draught of warmer air. The flying creature was returning!

"Freedom! Freedom!" sang the skylark in his alien voice as soon as he reached the frozen gathering and could see what had happened. "Congratulations, my friends, for putting an end to zat evil monster. Now let me lead you forward into ze light..." and he launched into the most dazzling song the frogs had ever heard. Inspired by this breakthrough, the skylark wished to convey to these tiny, frightened, ignorant folk all the wonders that awaited them. He sang of golden cornfields, ruby sunsets, waters that did not lie round and flat and still but shimmered away, twisting into the distance, flashing in all the colours of the rainbow. He told of countless different creatures: some small and brown with four legs; others that swam and disappeared only to jump out of the waters somewhere else; large, heavy creatures that ran over the fields and sleek, silver and glass cocoons that flashed and roared along their own looping pathways. It was fantastic, bewitching, frightening stuff.The skylark faltered. He saw round, dark, disbelieving eyes that only reflected the mud. "Ze colours... ze colours..." he repeated, stammering.

Too late he realised his mistake. The frogs closed around him: cold, grey, slimy and mud-covered things that hustled him backwards and prevented him from opening his wings. He began squawking in growing alarm.

It was a fearful struggle. The bird was much larger than any of the tiny frogs around it and it thrashed about desperately in an unknown, unpredictable way. But, like an insect, it was surprisingly lightweight for its size and could not recover once it was down in the mud. One after another its attackers kept coming until finally, it twittered its last.

The frogs drew back, once more mud-spattered and breathless. Once more they contemplated the awesome results of their actions, sprawled in front of them. Once more, a frozen silence descended. There were tears in Skippy's eyes.

"You mustn't cry, Skippy. We had to do it. The poor fool has served his purpose and it was only right to put him out of his misery." Bounder tried to comfort his friend. "C'mon now! Although he ranted and raved like a madman, he was right about one thing: The King had to go. Look – we're prisoners no more! Let's get started with our newfound freedom..."

Skippy nodded, swallowing her emotions. She turned away from the two dark, muddy shapes that were joined together in a cold embrace. Other friends came round to her and then, with a sigh, off into the puddles they splashed.

END

The group of listeners sighed.

"There's none so blind as those that will not see," commented one.

"But isn't that typical of all those who are supremely sure of the supremacy of their own community and who hate all immigrants or foreigners," said another.

"Yes. They are condemned to live in darkness," said Ivan.

"Ye shall seek the truth and the truth shall set you free," quoted David.

"If only it wasn't so difficult to seek it in the first place," replied Ana Maria. "I regret that many a prophet that brings new ideas into society has suffered that fate."

"But that was fascinating. Thank you for bringing your story to us," Hugo addressed the linguist.

"My pleasure," Abdul replied. "I tried to express the fear that I detect in others when they are confronted with a world outside their ken. It is easier to reject a foreign influence than to make the effort to try and understand it."

"I've found the same reaction!" said Ivan, the mathematician.

"Ancient maps carry warnings about uncharted regions," said one of the newcomers, a geographer. "Usually with some graphic illustration: 'Here there be dragons!' You know the sort of thing."

"Exploring the furthest reaches of the Earth. Trying to map the unknown. Travellers' tales of weird and wonderful monsters beyond our shores. How wonderful it all is! Well that must be where we go next," said Ana Maria. "Can you tell us more?"

"Now that we can map the world from space, and there are no more lost continents left to wonder about, I have to say geography these days has evolved into a subject that really puzzles me," said Hugo. "It seems such a jumble of other disciplines – geology, cartography, meteorology, environmental science, economic development... what is geography?"

"Well it does have an interdisciplinary focus, that's true," replied Hernando, the geographer. "I regard that as one of the subject's strengths. At its heart, though, it is all about a sense of place in space.

We are concerned with the distribution of humankind on the face of the Earth and how one party impacts on the other. Let me give you an example..."

Chapter 4

Geography: Road Transport

The Andes form the world's longest range of mountains. Starting in Tierra del Fuego at the tip of Antarctica, they run north in an uninterrupted chain up the backbone of South America until they reach the Caribbean Sea. This mighty cordillera is a natural barrier to east-west communication across the continent but where these mountains cross the equator and enter Colombia, the single spine forks into three, lower, less-impregnable walls.

The easternmost of these Colombian ranges broadens and – in the centre of the country – flattens into a long plateau of about 2,500 metres in height. In these tropical latitudes where parrots and monkeys might be expected to play, the plateau enjoys instead a pleasant, temperate climate that is not so very different from what you can find in Northern Europe.

A large fraction of Colombia's population lives on this plateau, which is dominated by the capital city: Santa Fe de Bogotá. A huge magnet, vibrant and chaotic, the city has drawn people in from all over the country – from valley and plain, mountain and jungle – to search for their fortune, to look for El Dorado, ever since the days of Columbus.

Rafael Silva and Juan Pablo Rodriguez were two such people: sitting at the back of an old Chevrolet bus as it clawed its way slowly up a twisting mountain road. For two days they had suffered the heat, sweat and carbon monoxide of their antiquated transport as it had juddered its way north-westward out of the selva, eventually rising now to refreshingly cooler climes. Inching their way up the mountain walls, the vegetation on either side of the bus was at last noticeably different: eucalyptus trees and pastureland had replaced bamboo bushes and banana plants.

But frustration was written all over Silva's dark, quick features. The journey to Bogotá could not pass rapidly enough for him, so eager was he to start his new life in the city.

"Hey, Juan Pablo! Couldn't you help fix this engine? Why don't you tell the driver to pull over and let you look at it? There must be a way to go faster than this."

The larger, slower man just grunted. He was content enough in his semi-slumber and had no great wish to dirty his hands on a machine that was too old and worn to transmit much more power to its buckled wheels. After many years working with vehicles of all shapes and sizes, the big man was wise enough to know which oily metalwork would respond to his testing fingers, and which would not.

Wandering slowly on bald tyres, the crowded bus climbed painfully round the next curve. Silva reckoned he knew every twist and turn of their route. Although he had not made this journey to the capital very often in his thirty years, he had an excellent spatial memory and he only had to travel along a road once and it was locked into his mind, drawn into a mental map that related it to all other features of the surrounding geography.

The next bend ahead, Silva recalled, was a tight, steep hairpin that undoubtedly would present problems to the ageing Chevrolet. The driver knew it too. The engine roared deep-throatedly and, belching black smoke, the old bus grumbled its way slowly forward – taking the easiest line it could find up the rising incline.

Suddenly, Rodriguez seemed to lurch out of his comatose state. Through the open window beside him he could hear the high-pitched whine of an approaching motor. Something was racing down the mountain road towards them. The big man glanced at his companion. His normally impassive face seemed to flicker a warning: Watch out!

It all happened very quickly. A sleek, low, silver saloon – driven too fast – burst into view round the corner. Its blacked-out windows gave no clue as to who was inside but, with tyres screaming on the disappearing road, the driver hit the brakes very late. The big, square-nosed Chevrolet, struggling upwards, slewed across the centre of the carriageway and the tight, right-hand curve gave no descending vehicle any room for manoeuvre. At the speed it was travelling, the saloon car could only avoid a head-on collision by opting to hit the outside of the bend. Blue smoke scorching from its tyres, it hit the outer fence with a BANG and in a split second it was gone. Out of sight; off the road; off the mountainside; gone.

The bus driver slammed both feet to the floor and, while pandemonium was breaking out in the interior behind him, he slowly backed his straining monster downhill, bumping it as close as possible into the mountain slope behind and beside him.

Passengers streamed out on to the roadway. Highly agitated, they clustered along the rim of tarmac where a large hole had been punched through some flimsy fence posts and the bushes behind. The ground tumbled away from them in a large brown scar down to a tangled stream some 100 metres below. There, half upside-down with its roof torn off like paper, lay a smoking wreck – one of its rear wheels still spinning.

Somebody was screaming: "Get them out; go down and get them out!"

"It's too late. Only God can help them now," another tersely replied.

The way down was slippery and dangerous, but one man started to descend. Then there came a sharp cough of ignition and the car was suddenly wrapped in flames. No one moved any more. In horror they all watched the heat build up and consume the crumpled debris of what had once been a fine vehicle. The only sounds were the crackle and roar of the fire and the broken weeping of some of those watching. There was nothing that could be done.

Rafael Silva turned away and walked over to the other side of the road – the centre of the hairpin. He leant against a rock and impatiently lit a cigarette. This was going to delay his journey even longer, he fumed. Puffing out smoke with a snort, his eyes were caught by the roadside above him: a large collection of car lights, headlamps and the occasional number plate was decorating the outside approach to the curve. They were littered all over a large shelf of rock on either side of a small, garishly-painted plaster Madonna that had been erected there. For any descending vehicle it was a clear warning that the bend ahead had already claimed a large number of victims.

"Crazy driver didn't know the road!" he scoffed, as his partner crossed towards him. "Obviously rich; with his hands on some fast Japanese sports model and thought the world belonged to him. Well he's got it all to himself now!"

"Korean," was the only comment his companion had to say.

The two men returned to the bus.

Three hours later and the Chevrolet arrived at its destination in Bogotá. It was now later in the day than had originally been planned, but the accident had occurred on the last serious bend before the road broke over the lip of the plateau and made its gentle descent into the city. Not much time had been lost. Police had arrived quite quickly to take statements from the bus driver and a couple of passengers. They had all moved off shortly afterwards. Silva never enquired as to the occupants of the car – with over seven million inhabitants in Bogotá, one or two less did not bother him in the slightest.

"Edificio Cartagena; Carrera 4A with Calle 106." The address had taken the two men to a wealthy part of the city and they stood there now, somewhat awed, before a tower block that soared fifteen floors above them. Juan Pablo Rodriguez took the folded paper from his companion and read the address slowly a second time, as if to reassure himself that they were now standing where they were supposed to be.

There was no mistake. The city's road network was laid out in a relentlessly logical manner with *carreras* running north-south and *calles* crossing them east-west. The calles started from No. 1 in the city's central plaza and increased in number going northward. Their destination was on street number 106. *Carreras* numbered off from the eastern edge of the city where it butted up against a long, low mountainous ridge, which projected above the plateau's surface. Carrera 4A was no distance from a thickly vegetated cliff face that came plunging down from goodness knows where above. The lower block facing them seemed to be carved directly out of this mountain slope.

"Well my cousin seems to have done alright for himself," said Silva. He had not seen him for a number of years, but he had heard that he was enjoying life. "I knew he had found some sort of success at last, but I didn't know how much. Let's go up and see."

There was strict security at the porter's lodge. Behind thick glass, a couple of gun-toting guards called up on the internal telephone to check out the visitors. Given clearance, large double-locked doors were opened and they waved the two men into the lobby. A high-speed lift zoomed them up to the 14th floor: residence of Señor Daniel Garcia.

"Daniel!" Silva sounded a whoop of greeting as soon as he spilled out of the lift.

He could not help noticing that as the door opened he was standing right in the centre of his cousin's apartment. The whole of the 14th floor was his.

"It has been a long time, eh? How have you been? Doing well, I guess. Driving trucks seems to have made you a bit of money by all appearances! Hey, meet my friend: Juan Pablo Rodriguez. He drives trucks too – when he gets out from being underneath them all the time."

Daniel Garcia laughed and prised himself away from his relation's enthusiastic embrace. "I don't just run trucks any more," he corrected. "I run the company. Pleased to meet you, Juan Pablo," he extended a hand to Rodriguez.

Greetings were extended into an offer of drinks and an escorted tour of the apartment. Garcia's family were introduced – a wife and a seven year old daughter glued to a television set – and then the two cousins exchanged news over where the last five years had taken them both. Rodriguez, as usual, said little, but kept his own counsel.

Clutching beers in front of a large picture window, with the city lights spread out in front and below them in the darkening night, talk eventually turned to business. Silva recounted how hard he had worked in the past; how responsible he was; how he had heard his cousin was making out in the truck business and even how he had gone and found a new driver-cum-mechanic who might be of use. So how about a helping hand to get started in the big city?

Garcia nodded, sipped his drink, and replied: "Well, Rafael, I can promise you some work in my office, but you will have to take what you find. As we have grown, there's something you can do in rationalising our transport schedules, but what exactly you can make of it I can't say. Get stuck in and see. As for Juan Pablo, I can always use help down at the depot. I'll introduce you to my chief driver and general fixer. There'll be no problem."

Silva beamed and shook his cousin's hand warmly. It was all settled. He knew it would work – with all this money surrounding his cousin there was bound to be some that could come his way. It was just a matter of time and seizing the right opportunity.

Bogotá's road network is clearly mapped out, but the traffic it has to support is horrendous. With no functioning rail system, all the city's commerce has to be conducted by road. In addition, with rising incomes the urban area is all the time growing in every direction: it was like living on a giant construction site. Huge cement mixers, dumper trucks, buses, private cars and more buses daily fight each other for access to the city's main thoroughfares. With all this movement, Bogotá's roads suffer a constant hammering that inevitably takes its toll. Potholes emerge almost overnight in even the most recently finished surfaces. The city's public authorities are in constant threat of losing the perpetual battle to fill in the holes faster than they appear. Roads occasionally have to be closed for emergency repair. For a newly-arrived truck driver paid to deliver his load on time, therefore, or his manager responsible for transport efficiency, trying to thread your way into the centre of the metropolis and out again is no easy matter. Both Silva and Rodriguez found their new work challenging.

They kept at it, however. Over the coming year their skills steadily improved – Rodriguez gained a reputation for solving just about any mechanical problem that came on wheels, and Silva could hustle a truckload of merchandise from anywhere in the city to anywhere else faster than anyone. Equipping all cabs with GPS tracking devices and two-way radios he kept abreast of hourly changes in traffic flow, road hold-ups or police check-points and could re-route deliveries in an instant. Customers were frequently delighted and some paid well over the odds for quick, efficient service that avoided delays, official bureaucracy and prying eyes.

Business was good, therefore, the company's profits were rising and the impatient Silva used his success to keep pestering his cousin for some action that would really pay back his enterprise in spadefuls. One day he got his chance.

"OK, Rafa. This is the big one you wanted," Daniel Garcia confided. "Only for the love of Jesus keep it quiet. We've got a consignment coming in for us on the south side and it needs to be delivered early tomorrow morning to the airstrip out on the Autopista Norte. It'll need two men. Pick your most reliable driver, take the maroon Toyota that I reserve for special journeys and get on to it. But absolutely no cock-ups, don't get stopped by anyone and on your mother's life don't let anyone look at what you're carrying. I'll get you the names of your contacts, addresses, times, everything. This is it, Rafa. Give it your hundred per cent undivided attention and we are talking *thousands* of dollars!"

Silva's heart leapt greedily: "How many thousands?" Airplanes and dollars meant only one thing – an illegal shipment of contraband to the USA.

"I guess we can make it five thousand between you and your driver, this time. And if all goes well and our clients are happy there may be many more. I'm trusting you on this one, Rafa. Don't let me down."

Five thousand dollars! Silva tried to stay calm. That was almost ten million pesos, and just for one trip across town.

Silva embraced his cousin. "Nothing to worry about. I'll take Juan Pablo Rodriguez – he's big, strong, and says nothing. And I know just about every back road and short cut in the city. The job's as good as done."

At 5.00am in the morning Rafael Silva arrived at the depot. Rodriguez was already there, checking over the Toyota. It was a 4.5 litre Land Cruiser pickup, converted Colombian style into a small truck. The back was built of horizontal wooden slats covered by a heavy black tarpaulin which was hooped over the top. From the rear it looked like a covered wagon as might be seen in an old Western. The substructure, however, was tough, mounted on 4-wheel drive and powered by a big engine that had clocked up only 12,000 kilometres so far. The two men climbed aboard and switched on. They were ready.

"There's a warehouse way over on 54 Sur with Carrera 27," said Silva. "We gotta pick up a load there and then make it up to Guaymaral aerodrome before 7.30am. There's *one thousand dollars* waiting for you if we get there on time." Silva grinned at his companion: "So c'mon, Juan Pablo, let's go."

The Toyota drove out into deserted streets just as the night was beginning to lighten.

There was little traffic about so the long drive across town was started quickly. Rodriguez was not even stopping for red lights.

"Take it easy, Juan Pablo!" Silva urged as they sped across another junction with barely a pause. "We don't want the police taking notice of us."

Rodriguez grunted but did not heed the advice. He was confident that there was no danger of being stopped yet – Bogotá traffic police were rarer than prostitutes at 5.30am in the morning. Silva blustered some more, but as his driver continued to ignore him he eventually lit a cigarette to hide his frustration and annoyance.

Crossing Bogotá from North to South is in some respects like taking a journey through South America. A variety of images bedazzle the senses: large, spacious, luxury houses hidden away behind walls and tall hedges contrast with street vendors sleeping under their stalls. Huge, imposing edifices belonging to internationally renowned banks and businesses stand next to the grinning *campesino*, or peasant, who tethers a cow on a temporarily unused, grassy construction site. And the people: even as the sun rises on a new day, many are already busy. Most are *mestizos* – of mixed blood – but amongst them the various racial types can be differentiated: stocky, dark-haired native Indians, a number of Negroes from the coast, and always a few Asians and those of European features. All mix freely with no overt prejudice but society here nonetheless follows the worldwide rule – the whiter the skin, the higher the economic standing. Latin American society, however, tends to be accepting of fate and is more intent on living, and enjoying, life to the full. At all times of the day and night, Latin rhythms can be heard emanating from one building or another in whatever street you pass. Music is in the blood.

Santa Fe de Bogotá was originally founded by the Spanish *conquistadores* in the sixteenth century. The city's history can still be partly seen in the beautiful, old, colonial style buildings arranged around the central plaza but this settlement now seems just a village overwhelmed by the energetic and ongoing expansion of modern Bogotá. Immediately to the north of the historical centre is the city's main business district: soaring steel and glass office blocks, five-star hotels, elegant shops and commercial centres. Further to the north lie the residential areas with luxury apartment blocks, parks, schools and private housing developments. Driving down through these areas, early in the morning with little traffic to bother you, can be a pleasurable experience. With a moist, temperate climate, the city supports plenty of oxygen-giving trees, shrubs and grass verges and steaming mists hang romantically over the verdant, plunging mountain wall that can be periodically glimpsed between the tower blocks. Even the pedestrians you encounter in the streets at this early part of the day have time to show their natural Colombian spontaneity and friendliness – before the numbers of cars and trucks build up to levels that seem to threaten their life and limb.

Moving deep into the southern half of the city brings you into the densely populated, largely unplanned sector where most of the urban newcomers have built their own accommodation, along with their businesses and livelihood. Public services are few and residents are thus dependent on their own resources. The Bogotanos' ingenuity is not lacking, however: numerous architectural styles and colours decorate the streets, recyclable materials have an imaginative array of uses and all sorts of informal businesses thrive.

Silva and Rodriguez drove south through increasingly poorer and poorer parts of town. There were no cars at all in this area now, only the occasional dilapidated truck and a large number of early walkers up and going about their business. At last, bumping over unmade roads, they approached a high adobe wall covered in graffiti. A small, dark woman of Indian blood was waiting for them beside two, large, rusty metal doors. From underneath a shabby blanket she unexpectedly produced a modern cell phone and began speaking into it. It was a most incongruous clash of cultures but it was certainly effective. Obviously obeying instructions, the woman turned her back and, fiddling with the padlock, unchained and opened the metal doors in front of the Toyota. She indicated to Rodriguez that he should reverse in and, this accomplished, she scuttled away into the interior and out of sight.

The two men backed their vehicle into the gloom beyond the gateway, cut the engine and got out. Silva went immediately to shut the metal doors in front of him and close off the outside world; Rodriguez meanwhile wandered round to the back of the truck – to where he had seen the woman disappear. A light clicked on. Emerging from behind a curtain the woman beckoned the two men forward to a huge pile of packages stacked in a corner.

"Jesus Christ!" exclaimed Silva. "We've got to take that? It'll never all fit in!"

Rodriguez opened the back of their truck and looked at the stockpile. It certainly wasn't going to be easy, but there was only one way to find out. He started loading.

Half an hour later, the two men were still at it. With the bulk of the truck full, they were now squeezing the packets into every little unfilled space they could find. The packets were all tightly wrapped in thick plastic and were of similar size and weight to a standard household brick. It was not easy to force them into holes that were not of the same dimension.

Silva was spluttering with frustration and irritation as the minutes ticked away. "Damn it all, Juan Pablo!" he swore at the steady, plodding routine of his bigger companion. "You've gotta move faster than that. Throw the rest of the stuff into the cab in front and let's get out of here. We've got less than an hour left!"

Swinging the big, metal doors open he waved the truck out on to the road. Desperately impatient, Silva leaped aboard, settled himself uncomfortably amongst numerous packages and urged his driver to go his fastest.

As they drove towards the centre of town the traffic built up rapidly. At 6.45am it was still early in the morning but it was not long before the laden truck encountered its first traffic jam. Pulling out from a side road on to Avenida 30, one of the main arteries of the city, there was a solid double line of vehicles unmoving in front of them.

"Shit no!" Silva screeched. "Don't join them. Drive straight across the centre reservation, turn left and we'll find another route. Go!"

Rodriguez dutifully forced his way across the stream of traffic, clunked the transmission into four-wheel drive and hauled the Land Cruiser up on to the centre reservation. Swaying under the load, they bounced down on to the opposite carriageway, straightened up and then slowly accelerated away from the crowds moving in the other direction. At the next junction, Silva directed them to the right and then they were bouncing over unmade roads again, kicking up clouds of dust as they weaved their way across a whole series of minor byways and back roads. At last they emerged on to another paved highway just as it joined a roundabout. The direction from here was not easy to judge but Silva, always carrying a map in his head, guessed they should bear left again. There was next to nothing on the road so Rodriguez put his foot down and in minutes they reached Carrera 68, a recognisable through-route with traffic moving swiftly along it.

Silva crowed in delight: "*Excellente!* It's all very simple! Just a matter of geography, getting about this city. Follow this road all the way round now until we hit the autopista. We should make it inside the hour now."

It was not going to be so easy, however. Entering into the stream of traffic, Rodriguez tried to accelerate into the gap behind a fast-moving car. Heavily laden, he was not going fast enough for a big truck bearing down behind them. Honking furiously, the truck drew closer, sitting right on their tail, before pulling out left to overtake. Suddenly, the car in front – with a twitch of its steering wheel – swerved wildly to avoid a large hole in the road. Rodriguez was not so lucky. Seeing it late he tried to do the same but, with the weight and speed at which they were travelling, the Toyota could not react sufficiently. A wheel hit the hole with a thump and their vehicle swayed madly. A second thump caught them almost immediately at the back and this time Rodriguez had to struggle with all his might to keep their crazy, leaping chariot on the road. They had bounced into the path of the truck behind.

Both trucks drew to a halt, Silva sweating with a whole complex of rage, fear and worry about what had happened. He loosed off a string of invective at his own driver before jumping out of the cab and rounding on to the other vehicle.

"You blind, stupid, incompetent sons of whores" – he didn't know who he was maddest at – "you nearly had me killed! Can't you keep your wheels on the road or must you try and crash into every other damn vehicle you see? You've got the wits and reactions of morons. You goddamned idiots!"

Both drivers inspected their respective vehicles while this tirade was going on. Fortunately, since the two trucks had been moving at almost the same speed when they met it had only been a glancing blow. A couple of wooden slats at the back of the Toyota had been splintered; the other truck was unmarked. Silva was not placated, however. He was becoming more and more offensive when he noticed that other cars were stopping to see what all the row was about. A traffic jam was building up rapidly all around them. Somewhere at the back a policeman was dismounting from a motorbike. Through the red mists of his rage he realised this was the last thing he wanted. Swearing volubly he turned to inspect what damage had been done to his valuable cargo. As he lifted the black tarpaulin, what met his eyes turned his blood to ice and decided him to get out of the place as quickly as possible. Wooden splinters had pierced some of the packets that had been squashed in at the back of the load and a trickle of white powder was now cascading down through the truck and on to the tarmac.

Leaping as if stung, he hollered at Rodriguez to get back into the cab and start the engine. Meanwhile, grappling under the tarpaulin at the back, he tried to pull apart the splintered woodwork and patch up the damaged packages. There was no time for anything but rudimentary repair work. Still sweating and swearing profusely he ran back to join his partner as the truck slowly began to pull away.

"Go! Go! Go! For Christ's sake move this damn wagon!" he ordered. As they gathered speed he put his head forward and peered into the wing mirror to see what was happening behind. The policeman was sauntering up, looking bored, to the spot they had just vacated. Silva just prayed that he would not notice anything unusual.

For the next half-hour the two men sat in silence, the more nervous one breathing more easily the further and further they drove without mishap. Once, whilst stopped at more traffic lights, Silva got out and raced round to the back for a quick inspection. No telltale trail of white powder was visible. To great relief he resumed his position in front and they continued their journey.

At 7.15am Silva's cell phone beeped. It was Daniel Garcia, calling from the office:

"Where are you guys? There are people waiting at Guaymaral."

"Take it easy. We're on the autopista right now and we should get there in the next quarter hour or so. But why the hell didn't you tell us it was such a big load?" Silva demanded. "We needed more time and a bigger truck to pack it all in."

"You haven't left any behind, have you?" Garcia was suddenly very serious.

"No, no, *tranquilo*! We've got it all, but it has taken us longer than expected. Can the plane wait?"

"Not really. Just get there!" Garcia hung up.

That was it: destination confirmed and all was ready. Despite scares, they were on schedule and moving steadily towards their goal. Silva relaxed and, with a slight smile, began thinking about all the money he was going to make. Four thousand dollars... not bad for a morning's work. He looked sideways at Rodriguez: solid, impassive, his big hands guiding them now in the middle lane of the highway. One thousand for him – though I'm damned if he deserves it, Silva thought, especially after nearly wiping us out earlier.

The clouds were lowering as, at last, the Toyota turned off the autopista and followed the deserted side road that led to the aerodrome. At precisely 7.35am they were driving across the level grass towards the hangar that contained the small, twin-engine executive airplane that was waiting for them.

Silva and Rodriguez were greeted by two dark-suited, unsmiling men and, after brief introductions had been made, all four started transferring the load into the plane. They formed a line and, passing packages one to the other, they quickly began to fill the cramped space at the back of the aircraft. Then Silva's cell phone beeped again.

"Where the Christ are you?" It was Garcia again, only he sounded highly agitated.

"We're loading the plane right now."

"What the hell have you been doing? The police have got a general call out for you. Half the damn city is on alert looking for the truck. They've got your number plate, a brief description and they know you're hauling cocaine. What did you do – send them an invitation to the party??"

Silva's mind went numb. He tried to burble a reply but Garcia cut him short.

"Look, don't give me any crap. Just make sure the plane takes off with all the load on board and then get as far away from the airfield as you can. No one knows where you are just yet but the truck is hot and you've got to hide it before someone catches up with you. If you do get caught then you don't know me; you've been on the other side of town all the time and you've never seen an aircraft in your life. But don't get caught. If you want to hang on to your balls, don't get caught. You and the Toyota have just got to disappear where no one will find you. Gettit?"

Silva's brain was paralysed. "Yeah, yeah," he mumbled, "we'll hide… but where? What are we gonna do?"

The cell phone went quiet for a few seconds as Garcia thought furiously. He had more to lose than his cousin if things went awry: he had to extricate them from the mess they had got themselves into.

"There's a workshop you can go to which can fix up the truck so that no one will recognise it. The owner is reliable. I'll phone him and warn him to expect you. It's on Carrera 33 with 3, right down near the centre. Understand? But first of all make sure that plane takes off safely: we're all dead meat otherwise… and I'm not talking about what the police will do to you. On 33 with 3. OK? Get there and stay out of sight while you do so. Don't foul up, Rafa. If you know your way round the city like you say you do, then come through for me, OK? Do it!"

Silva pocketed the cell phone and put his face in order. He breathed deep and slow. Despite the rise and fall of his stomach, he came to the realisation that they were relatively safe at the moment, hidden away in the hangar, and his first priority was to get the plane into the sky with its full complement of cargo. Acting as calmly as possible, he rejoined the others in transferring the load.

With four people working at it, it did not take long to finish packing the aircraft. Silva ran a quick check over the truck and ensured that the two unsmiling men were satisfied with everything. Stepping back out of the way, he and Rodriguez watched as the two men boarded the plane, taxied out on to the airfield and, with engine roaring, sped away across the grass, into the distance and finally up, up into the darkening clouds.

It was now time to move: to run the gauntlet into the city centre. Turning to Rodriguez, Silva waved the cell phone at him and found himself getting angrier and angrier with every word he spoke:

"The police are on to us! Thanks to you hitting that truck earlier, they saw what we were carrying and now they're searching the city for us. We can apparently ditch this wagon in a hideaway on 33 with 3 – but we've got to get there first!"

Desperation and fear for his life turned Silva's voice to a venomous whisper:

"Can you drive, Rodriguez? Without hitting anything this time? Without the police picking us up? You'd better… you're a dead man otherwise."

Rodriguez's expression did not change. It drove Silva wild to see it, but such threats seemed to have absolutely no impact on the man. His face was a blank screen: maybe he hadn't heard correctly? Or was he so stupid the words had no meaning? He could move, however: he walked over to the cab of the Toyota, got in and started up the engine.

"What was that address?" he asked Silva as soon as the other joined him. The voice was flat, emotionless. It was like some thick-skinned, big ox talking.

"Calle 33 with Carrera 3, down near the centre," the smaller man growled, barely concealing his fury.

They left the airfield and turned south, heading into the city on a minor, unmade road parallel to the autopista. It started to rain. Neither man spoke any more.

In some places on Earth, moving around on the surface of the planet presents no problem. Humankind has evolved a relationship with the immediate environment which facilitates rapid transport and efficient intercommunication. Even where the physical structure of the globe presents formidable problems to the passage of man, human ingenuity has risen to the challenge and found sophisticated and technologically impressive solutions: towering bridges, lengthy tunnels, super-highways, etc. In other places, however – even where the physical geography is relatively friendly – the relationship that has evolved between people and the environment has been less successful in providing for movement. This is particularly true where there are dense concentrations of humanity and social organisation has been lacking. Here communal endeavours are swamped by ever-increasing numbers of individuals.

Bogotá city centre at 8.00am on weekday mornings is such a place. Long lines of traffic build up on all major highways and movement anywhere is frustratingly slow – and if it pours with rain it gets worse. This was the experience of Rafael Silva and Juan Pablo Rodriguez. Trying to find an uninterrupted vein into the heart of the metropolis was not at all easy. Their first option was a potholed, single-track, dirt road that zigzagged its way past old farms and acres of glasshouses on the edge of the city. Although progress was slow, it was steady and the intensifying rain brought a welcome benefit: Ignoring his partner's uncompre-hending glare, Rodriguez stopped the Toyota and, risking saturation, methodically removed the black tarpaulin from the rear of the truck. He guessed correctly that the rain would wash away any incriminating evidence of their original cargo.

Bumping and splashing their way onward, the two men could not avoid the traffic for much longer. Mud-splattered after their circuitous route on unmetalled roads, they eventually met up with a diagonal avenue that redirected them back to the autopista. They then emerged into a slow-moving train of vehicles gradually shunting its way southward.

It was just a matter of time now before they met up with the police. Silva squirmed nervously in his seat, his eyes everywhere, peering through the rain, with fogged-up side windows and rear mirrors, to try and spot any police car before it got close. Rodriguez was unflappable: trusting to luck, poor visibility and the Toyota's mud-disguised and changed appearance to get them through.

It seemed to work at first. Concealed amongst countless other grey trucks fighting their way through the rush-hour crowds, the Toyota gradually drove further and further into Bogotá's centre. The autopista was actually an excellent hiding place in such conditions – no highway patrol could overtake them and in the police checkpoints they passed there was no one interested in standing out in the downpour to scrutinise the endless chain of commuting motors.

To turn left, eastward, off the three-lane highway they were on, Rodriguez had to take a slipway that led to a bridge across the autopista. Silva thus directed them on to Calle 100, meaning to move in a series of eastward/southward steps to his intended destination of Calle 33 with 3. They were now in the wealthy boulevards of the city, with large stores, commercial centres and hotels about them. The traffic was no easier. A police car appeared by the corner of a large fashion wear shop as the traffic lights changed, but it seemed to take no notice of them. Silva's pulse raced but then relaxed. They moved on.

Another right then left and they were on Calle 92 with Carrera 11: a block nearer, now amongst elegant furniture stores. Despite the rain, a traffic cop buzzed across in front of them on his motorbike. In this city, with this weather, most of his ilk would have been resting up under shelter, swapping stories and letting the traffic jams slowly sort themselves out. This one was different, however: in his manner, busy, confident and obviously determined to get things done. There is always one!

As Rodriguez drew up behind a yellow taxi in the queue in front of him he saw the policeman eyeing the Toyota. The cars in front had just started to move again when the cop turned his bike with the obvious intention of coming to investigate further. Rodriguez decided not to wait – at the next junction he took the line with the least traffic and accelerated north on a small side road between tall apartment blocks. Swerving to avoid a rank of parked cars, he ploughed through a river of collected rainwater and then swiftly spun the wheel to the right and entered another residential street. Silva had his eyes glued to the rear view mirror and saw the cop following behind them, slowing down to negotiate the flooded corner they had just left. Accelerating hard, Rodriguez came roaring up to the next block, turned left and, forcing his way past a couple of surprised cars coming towards him, turned left again into another quiet, rain-washed street. Seeing a big, blue Ford pickup approaching he suddenly jammed on all his brakes hard, pulled in tight to the left-hand side of the road and came splashing and sliding to a halt.

The traffic cop on his motorbike had seen his quarry rapidly disappearing and, suspicions aroused, came speeding after. He came round the first block, with no trouble and, expecting to see the mud-splattered truck some distance ahead, took the second corner as fast as he dared. To his horror, the cop was confronted with a big, blue wagon that was overtaking on his side of the road and coming straight at him. The flooded road gave no grip to the two spinning wheels that were trying to brake. The pickup was fortunately not going very fast but with a crash the motorbike clipped the wing of the Ford and the policeman took off, cartwheeling through the air.

Rodriguez did not wait to see the outcome. Slamming the Toyota back into gear he accelerated away, leaving the motorbike sprawled across the road in front of the pickup and the policeman groaning on the wet tarmac some distance away. At the end of the block he turned left again and disappeared from the scene, heading south once more en route for their goal.

Silva burst into voice, not knowing whether to praise or condemn his partner:

"My God! Why did you have to go and cause an accident? Now this place will be crawling with police..."

"Nothing to do with us," grunted Rodriguez in reply, guiding the truck past the next set of traffic lights.

The two men returned to the main streets, losing themselves in the stream of vehicles slowly moving across town. Within minutes they passed a police car, sirens screaming, forcing its way through the congestion heading in the direction they had just left. Moments later they passed another. But now they were streets away and just another drab, dishevelled truck amongst many. Without further incident to delay them they soon reached Carrera 5, close by the mountain wall of the city, and started counting off the roads south: Calle 76, five minutes later – Calle 53, then 39.

But there was something not quite right – the closer they got the more unlikely this neighbourhood appeared to be. This was not a district full of workshops, stores and small industry. Silva began to get fidgety. There was also an uncomfortably high presence of green-uniformed troops and other military personnel about. At last they got there: Calle 33. Rodriguez turned off and slowly motored uphill towards the heavily wooded cliff face that seemed to fill the windscreen. But where was their destination? There was a church and a large cemetery where Carrera 3 was supposed to be.

Silva reached for the cell phone. His cousin was out of the office so it took him a little while before he could get through, by which time he was thoroughly disturbed:

"Where's this hideaway, Daniel? We are here on 33 and there's a cemetery where Carrera 3 should be!"

"What? Where are you??"

"On Calle 33 looking for this workshop you mentioned."

"That's on *Carrera* 33 with 3, *estupido*! Don't you know the geography of this city yet? You're on the wrong side of town from where I sent you… Christ! If you're up where you say you are then you must be in the middle of the military complex. Get the hell out of there…"

For the second time that morning, Rafael Silva was dumbstruck. Seconds ticked away while his mind reeled in fear and confusion. The world seemed to be slowly turning upside down and filling up with icy cold mists that were gripping his soul. Far from a safe hideaway, he was in the middle of the greatest danger! How could that have happened? He roared obscenities in the close confines of the cab in the attempt to regain his composure. The dry, patient tones of his cousin speaking through the earpiece came filtering back into his consciousness:

"Forget the workshop. Just get out of there. From where you are, stay high and find your way round the eastern rim of the city until you hit the old Villavicencio road going south. Got that? I'll come back to you later when I've got something fixed up. Can you manage that? Can you stay out of trouble?"

"Yeah, yeah," Silva lied. "No one's interested in us. Everything's gone fine, Daniel. The plane took off no problem and the truck's clean." He was worried that he might lose some of the money he had been promised.

"The truck is *not* clean, Rafa," his cousin corrected him. "I reported it stolen by persons unknown, early this morning, soon after we heard the police were looking for it. They have the number plate and so it was important to tell them first before they got to us. Like I said, Rafa, get out of town and don't get stopped."

The phone went dead.

"Damn! Damn! Damn!" Silva beat his hands on the dashboard, his knees and his companion's shoulder. Rodriguez barely flinched. Hearing only one-half of the conversation he did not know what had gone wrong, but from the extravagant explosion beside him he knew they had somehow passed the workshop.

"Where now?" he asked.

"Head south and take the Villavicencio road outta Bogotá," came the scowling reply.

Silva was full of fury. He hated mistakes; he hated the big, calm, unflappable Rodriguez; but most of all he hated the possibility of losing any of the money he had been promised.

It took another tense half-hour to circle round the mountainous edge of the city and eventually meet up with traffic moving into the centre from the south side. In this time, communication between the two men was strained, but when Rodriguez finally found out that their number plate was known to the police he promptly came up with the solution. Pulling over beside a beat-up old Renault parked on rough ground, the big man got out of the cab, bent down by the smaller car and in seconds his strong fingers had prised off its registration plates. Driving off quickly, he stopped a kilometre further on and, producing a roll of adhesive tape, strapped his newly-acquired plates on top of the Toyota's. He trusted to the rain and general gloom that his work would go unnoticed. He was not wrong.

At last the two men found themselves moving faster, against the rush, on a road that they knew well enough: it was the same route that had carried them into the city over a year ago when they had first come seeking their fortune.

Silva was praying that that fortune would soon be falling into his hands. He was waiting impatiently for his cousin to call. As soon as the cell phone beeped he had it by his ear.

"Rafael? Still safe? Fine." Garcia sounded content. "Look, I've left a car for you, just off the road, some way out of town. There's a package on the back seat that you'll need, but take care – it's explosive! Put the package in the Toyota, switch to the car I've left for you and I'll meet you in Villavicencio. Do everything I say

73

and everything will be fine."

Silva listened keenly. From the relaxed tone of his cousin's voice it sounded like he had had contact with the client and payment was confirmed. They only had to cover their traces now and their worries would be over. The changed identity of the Toyota had so far eluded detection and if it was burnt out on some lonely rubbish dump then that state of affairs would be permanent. Daniel Garcia repeated the details once more and Silva ensured he had it all straight. This time there were going to be absolutely no flaws, no misunderstandings, no mistakes, to deny him his fortune.

It was a blue-grey Hyundai, low and sleek, and it was hiding out of sight from the main road on a rough track behind some old farm buildings. Rafael Silva was on his knees, looking underneath for a flattened beer can that supposedly contained the keys he required. For a brief, panic-stricken moment, scrabbling in the dirt, Silva thought that he was never going to find it; that someone else had got there first; or that they had never been put there originally. Then his outstretched hand touched something that rattled. With great relief he stood up clutching his prize and proceeded to clean himself down. He looked around. No one could be seen – except for Rodriguez busy backing the Toyota underneath the tall trees that fringed the path behind him.

Within seconds Silva was in the driving seat of the car, stretching out and enjoying the luxury of the brand-new machine. It was supremely comfortable, it looked fast and it spoke to him of a lifestyle that he had always wanted. For the time being he basked in the illusion that this was his car. He ran his hands caressingly over the steering wheel. But how could he have one of his own? Permanently? He had to make more money. Turning, he saw a large attaché case on the back seat that the car's blacked-out windows had prevented him from noticing before. He reached across. Careful! He knew what it contained... Slowly a thought came to him: a way of making an extra thousand dollars quickly. An explosive thought... Yes, five thousand dollars was an altogether preferable sum to only four thousand. And it was what he deserved anyway. For a few seconds he mulled the idea over, working it all through. Then he got out of the car and walked purposefully over towards the truck. Whistling.

"Hey, Juan Pablo! Can you come and check over this car for me? Daniel tells me that it needs tuning up – maybe the timing is a little out?" Silva escorted his companion from one vehicle to the other, chattering all the time:

"Daniel's got everything arranged. We are to drive these two wagons down to meet him in Villavicencio and there he'll take over and pay us off. I'll go first in this car and you follow on five minutes later in the truck. OK? But make sure this fancy machine is functioning perfectly will you? Daniel said he's had problems with it. Meanwhile, I'll leave the address you need on the Toyota's dashboard."

Silva waited until his driver was well and truly immersed in the entrails of the new motor before he fetched out the attaché case from the back seat and, making sure that he kept the car and his own body obstructing Rodriguez's line of sight at all times, he carried the case back over to the truck. Working quickly, he climbed into the cab and then clicked round the combination lock on the case to read: 950 – nine minutes, fifty seconds before it blew up. He pulled out a mess of old papers and maps behind the driver's seat, slipped the attaché case into the gap behind that was revealed and promptly replaced the papers to cover it all up again. Scribbling a fictitious address on a bit of paper, he left it just above the steering wheel and then returned unhurriedly to the other vehicle. Rodriguez was now underneath and fumbling about below the Hyundai's engine and had not noticed anything.

A minute later and the big man emerged from below the car

and, his eyes returning to the front of the vehicle, he grunted to his partner:

"Right! Try her now."

Silva slipped into the driving seat without delay and switched on. The engine hummed faultlessly, as he knew it would. Secretly, he would not have minded if it had leaped and thumped about like a kangaroo, he only wanted to get away now as quickly as possible. Trying to keep his impatience under tight control, Silva brought the window down and inclined his head towards the other:

"Just perfect, Juan Pablo." He flashed a smile. "You've done a great job. Now: give me a few minutes to get away and then follow on after. You should recognise the road well enough… I'll see you next in Villavicencio, with a couple of beers waiting for you! OK? Great!"

Silva put the car in gear and, pulse racing, he slowly eased his way over the rutted path down to the main road. Making every attempt not to hurry, he paused and looked back to wave generously to the large, impassive man watching him. He waited just long enough to see Rodriguez turn and walk back to the truck and then he put his foot down and pulled out on to the Villavicencio road.

Silva was grinning all over his face as he accelerated away. He reckoned that only four minutes remained now before the case exploded, igniting the petrol tank and burning out the Toyota and everything in it. Poor, stupid Rodriguez would not know what hit him. He was sitting on top of a bomb that he knew nothing about. Such a thick-headed driver! All the telephoned conversations with Daniel he would not have understood. But it was a good idea to get rid of him: another driver with a bit more intelligence and a little less dumb insolence could easily be found to take his place, and the fewer people who knew what had happened this day would be better. He was sure his cousin would approve. You could never be too safe.

The car sped along the deserted road faster and faster as Silva gloated over what he had done. It was sheer delight handling such a powerful and responsive machine. And this was only the first part of the payoff that he would be receiving for all his hard work. Five thousand dollars was waiting for him less than an hour away, with the promise of more to come in the future. Maybe he could keep this car for a bit longer into the bargain? He was sure his cousin could extend the loan.

Such dreams were threatening to carry Silva away. In a few moments, however, he would reach the lip of the plateau and start the descent down the twisting road to the hotter climate below. Silva's map-like mind had not forgotten the lay of the land and, despite the excitement of all he had achieved, he eased up on the accelerator as he approached the first serious bend that took him over the edge of the mountainside.

A garishly painted, plaster Madonna littered about with discarded car lights could be seen decorating the rock face at the side of the road below him. Silva recognised it at once and hit his brakes with purpose.

Nothing happened!

Panicking immediately, he stamped both his feet down hard.

Still nothing! What was wrong?

The car was now descending like a bullet and was completely out of control.

It was a brand new car – it had to work!

The edge of the curve loomed in front.

Rodriguez had only just checked it all over…

Silva lunged at the hand brake and found that that too offered no resistance.

Rodriguez!!!

His mind was screaming in fear when he ran out of road. He hit the outer fence with a BANG and in a split second he was gone. Out of sight, off the mountainside: gone, gone, gone.

Juan Pablo Rodriguez stopped the bus and got down some seventy metres or so above the curve. He waved the crowded old Chevrolet goodbye and then walked along the short distance to where he noticed a large hole that had been punched through the newly-erected wooden fence that lined the rim of the road. Standing on the edge of the tarmac, he peered over the side and nodded slowly with grim satisfaction at what he could see below. A blue-grey saloon that had obviously once been a fine machine was burning fiercely, upside down, in a tangled gully vertically beneath him. On closer inspection, a number of other rusting wrecks could be clearly seen all around – some of them years old and almost hidden in the undergrowth. The remains of the Hyundai was merely the latest addition, and Rodriguez guessed that, with over seven million inhabitants in Bogotá and far too many cars on its crowded roads, nobody would lose much sleep over the loss of this one.

He continued his walk down the mountain road, keeping well to the side when he heard any fast-moving car coming, and waited for the next bus that might pass his way. Two burnt-out vehicles were behind him now and that might be a little difficult to explain to Daniel Garcia but, as they had already agreed on the cell phone that Rodriguez had found left behind in the Toyota, Silva was an arrogant, impatient man and his knowledge of geography was not as good as he thought it was.

END

"Ouch! That really is a tale of the impact of man on the Earth," commented Abdul.

"I like it: an essay on spatial relations and the perils of losing your way," said Ana Maria.

"Yet the urge to travel and explore is a basic truth of all humankind," said David, the philosopher. *"We evolved from our ape ancestors simply by leaving the forests behind us and taking those first upright steps into the wider world. Getting lost is the risk we have to*

take if we want to go forward."

"So where do we go next?" asked Hugo. "After exploring the Earth, where does that lead us now?"

"Through time," said Ivan. "Humankind travelling through space is one dimension; through time is the other. History!"

"His story!" said Ana Maria. "It says it all! Let me go find someone I know who can help tell that. I'll be back as soon as I can."

The party was steadily growing in number and the interest generated was growing with it. Ana Maria shortly returned on the arm of Jeroen, a distinguished, grey-bearded gentleman who carried a twinkle in his eye. She had already told him of what the group was up to and her older partner was composing his thoughts as he arrived on the balcony.

"What is history, you ask" he began. "Well let me first tell you what it is not. The popular conception that it is some list of facts and events that exist objectively and independently of the interpretation of the historian is a complete fallacy. History is shaped by the very process of studying it. It is not about what happened in the past. It is what we create today from random data that we pick up from days gone by."

"Thank you," said the philosopher. "You have reinforced what we were saying earlier. It is the search for patterns that we find makes sense to us."

"Indeed. We sample written evidence that we can find in the records of various institutions and draw our arguments, our conclusions, from those. Generally speaking, the further back we go, the more scarce the written record, the wider the possible interpretation that can be placed on how all the bits fit together. It is like trying to imagine what a past building might have looked like when only a few bricks can be found. There are many possible outlines."

"Are there any universal truths that can be derived from our past, can you tell us that?" asked Hernando.

"It is my opinion, I regret to say, that the only truth we learn from history is that we never learn from history," said their guest. "Let me enlarge upon that truth..."

Chapter 5

History: Environmental Impact

Tourism is a fast-expanding industry. There is hardly anywhere on Earth that has not already been touched by some group of visitors busily holidaymaking. From the high Andes to the centre of the Sahara desert, no condor or camel can relax in peace these days without being surprised by a camera-clicking, Coke-toting posse of eager tourists.

Nothing that was fashionable yesterday will do for today, of course. The modern culture-vulture has to impress his neighbours with photographs of places ever-more distant, colourful, exclusive.

It is a big business, naturally, catering for such a demanding clientele. Tour companies vie with one another to provide more unique holiday packages every year, with all the latest, state-of-the-art transport technologies to whisk the time-pressured tourist from each fascinating destination to the next. Every day must be packed full with twenty-four hours of diverse entertainment. No place that was seen last year... oh no... and no time, please, to waste languishing in airport lounges or hotel receptions waiting for connections to the next, not-to-be-missed delight.

Perhaps it is just as well that there is this unceasing rush to move on to the next novelty and never go back to where one has been before because who wants to see the impact of what tourism leaves behind? It is not very pleasant. Piles of old Coke and beer cans, plastic yoghurt pots, sandwich wrappers and hamburger cartons: detritus of instant lunches, instantly forgotten. And local colour? It comes now in technicolour T-shirts on idle street corners bedazzled by quick commercialism; traditional costume and custom all but a memory.

Yes: tourism is a fast-moving business and there is no profit and no prizes for those who get left behind.

"Where shall we go this time?" asked Veronica Vultura, pouting over the photographs of their holiday last year. "After diving down to the bottom of the Caribbean and shooting up beyond the stratosphere with space shuttles what else is there to do?"

Her husband Victor was silent. He scanned slowly through one travel programme after another, searching each website intently. He stopped at one lurid display for several minutes. At last he snorted one word: "History!" and stood up. The decision had been made.

Veronica moved across to see what he had been looking at.

"The very latest in ethnic experiences," the caption blared out at her. "Take your place in the crowd at any Time you choose! See History unfold right in front of you! Rush now to book up this fabulous offer."

The company logo of *Time Travel Tours* was blazoned across the computer screen.

"The fashion now is minimal environmental impact," explained the Time Travel Tours agent enthusiastically. "We have the technology to put you folks back into any period of the past you choose but we can't have you interfering with History, now can we?"

He smiled patronisingly. "Nope! Time Travel Tourists must melt into the crowd, look just like everyone else of that period, *be* like everyone else. The ultimate in ethnicity! You'll love it!" He paused. An eyebrow raised quizzically: "Just what era in history were you thinking of visiting?"

Victor hesitated. "Er, somewhere classical, I guess. Biblical times. Yeah, Bethlehem. How about the Birth of Christ? Wouldn't you like that, Vera?" he turned to his side.

His wife smiled brightly and batted her eyelids. "Oh, gee, yes," she cooed. "The Babe in the manger... I bet he looks just *adorable*..."

The tour official frowned. "Bit difficult, that one. Everyone accounted for, you see. Animals in the stables, shepherds, three kings; where would we fit in two extras? I'm *very* sorry, sir, but we can't do you for that one."

He thought quickly. "How about the Crucifixion? Pretty big event too, you know, historically speaking. And large crowds to place you in as well. Yessir! A must. We have lots of biblical robes from our props department to clothe you in – you'd both look great in Jerusalem."

"But… but can't I wear my pink lycra bodysuit?" Veronica wailed. "I've just bought it. And I *do* want to swim in the Sea of Galilee if I'm going there…"

"I do understand, madam, and of course we *can* arrange that. But not just at the time of the Crucifixion, if you can wait a little. First we'll have you in the crowd scene – like extras in a film set, you know – and then we'll bring you out of that era and into a period a little more appropriate for swimming or whatever else you want to do." He beamed. "Haven't you always wanted to be a film star? And this is even better. I know you'll just *love* the Crucifixion. Now if you'd like to sign on the line there… Thank you!"

"Aw, c'mon, honey," Veronica complained, "do we really have to learn all this Ancient Hebrew stuff?"

"You heard what the man said, Vera," her husband replied. "When in Jerusalem, do like the Jews. We gotta look and talk like everyone else. And besides, it's only a few words we have to learn."

"Yeah I guess you're right. It's just that I was never much good at foreign languages. What's this word anyway? *Brabass*? How do I say that?"

"It's a name of sumfin or other. We gotta shout it out like all the rest, the tour guide said. Gee, it is kinda exciting; better'n being in a film set, even."

"'*Crucify him!*' I sure hope I don't foul that one up," Veronica worried. "This is a big occasion an' I don't wanna make a fool of myself in front of all those people. You're gonna stay right close, aren't you? Just imagine if I got lost in the crowd... whatever would I do? It would be just *awful!!*" Her eyes grew round with fear and she shook a mass of dark brown curls at her husband.

"Don't worry, honey. You'll do just fine I know – and I'll be right back of you all the time. Now let me fix your hair here..." Victor sprayed a little more 'SupaNatural Hair Gloss' over her carefully casual hair arrangement. It was time to get ready to go.

The tour official met them at the edge of town as arranged. He carried a clipboard and a travel bag and he was smiling a welcome as the Vulturas drove up.

"Leave the motor just there, that's right," he called out as Victor and Veronica climbed carefully out into the morning sun. "Mrs Vultura, you look simply *divine*. Didn't I say we had just the right costumes for you? Now shake the creases out here, sir," he fussed over Victor, "we can't have you looking as if you've been sitting down all day, now can we? Detail! We gotta think of every detail."

The buildings around them were all large, grey, uninteresting warehouses. The tour guide led the way quickly to the nearest, his two companions following hurriedly, rather embarrassed to be out in the open wearing such strange garments. A door opened into a small lobby. Inside were two other couples dressed in similar clothing to the Vulturas and all waiting in an atmosphere of anxiety mixed with high excitement.

"Welcome, welcome everyone," the travel courier opened his arms expansively. "Mr and Mrs Vultura, meet your fellow companions on this trip: the Canns, Tim and Tina, and Phil and Phyllis Stein. All ready? Great. Just walk this way, please."

The door on to the main floor of the warehouse was opened. There, just a short distance away, waited what looked like an old greyish-white plaster and adobe building. On closer examination it turned out to be just that and no more – except that this unassuming cube-shaped structure concealed within it a mass of gleaming black and silver machinery.

The courier held aside a rickety wooden door so that all could enter. Beside all the machinery there was just enough room for the seven people to squeeze in, standing close to one another. Veronica looked down at the computer screens and silver dials arranged around her. *"You're always on time with Time Travel Tours,"* one caption blinked at her. *"Never a moment wasted!"*

"This is our Mark III time capsule," the courier announced proudly, "pre-programmed for Jerusalem, some two thousand years ago. A final check now and we are on our way."

He glanced first down a list on his clipboard and then looked keenly at each face of the tourists.

"Hmmm. I like the beards, gentlemen. It's remarkable how they grow in just a few days, don't you think? We can't look too close-shaven, can we? Detail, detail! No watches visible? Good, good. And no cameras? Absolutely not! Now: here… we… GO!"

A lever was pulled down and a sequence of buttons pressed. Everything went instantly black and three couples clung breathlessly together as the darkness whirred around them.

A silent, numbing void… Nothingness… a moment which stretched out to embrace all Time.

Suddenly light flooded the tiny building. All seven passengers blinked rapidly as their eyes became accustomed to the dazzling new spectacle that now appeared before them. An olive-green Mediterranean hillside rose up beyond them on one side; a collection of whitish plaster and adobe buildings greeted them on the other.

"Jerusalem!" gasped Tina Cann.

"Wait a second, let's check that," responded the courier efficiently.

He touched a keyboard nearby and a computer screen shone the message: "Jerusalem, circa 0030 AD, countdown to

Crucifixion 5 hrs, 15 mins, 20 secs."

"Just in time!" happily beamed the Time Travel Tours company guide. "You can always be sure of up-to-the-minute service if you go with us. Now if you have read our carefully planned programme itinerary for today you will see that you should walk downtown to the main square this morning to attend the big public meeting and then afterwards come back up here and beyond to Calvary. That's the big hill behind us... don't worry Mrs Vultura, you can't miss the place. It'll be marked with three big crosses. Just follow the crowds, it'll be easy. When it's all over I will meet you back here again. Now, off you go and grab a slice of History. Have a nice day!"

It was, indeed, remarkably easy. The Time Travel capsule sat on the outskirts of Jerusalem just like any other of the buildings of the town. All around people were emerging from their white plaster homes and, in ones and twos, were slowly moving down the stony pathways into the centre. It was not at all difficult for the tourists to slip out unnoticed and join the throng.

People kept arriving from every side. As Victor stumbled along he was reassured to notice that others appeared to have as much difficulty as he in hurrying over the stones in open-toed sandals. No one seemed to be talking at all: heads were down, the mood was sombre, expectant. The only sound was the shuffling of hundreds of feet over the broken pathways. There was a sudden scream – instantly stifled – as one woman tumbled into the dirt in her hurry. It was all somehow immensely exciting.

Victor and Veronica had already lost sight of their companions – they were indistinguishable from everyone else – but at last they arrived at the back of a densely packed square and there, with a thrill, they saw for the first time real Roman soldiers ordering people about, trying to hold back the gathering mass. Over the heads of everyone, down at the front of the square, stood an imposing building with four columns supporting a balcony. Somebody was up there, talking to the front ranks of the crowd.

"Who's the guy wearing the bathrobe?" hissed Veronica, as they moved forward.

"It's a Roman toga, dummy!" Victor whispered back. "Dunno who it is… maybe Julius Caesar or someone…"

"What's he saying?" Veronica was desperate to communicate with her husband. They had been silent all along for fear of being overheard in the crowd but she could hold it back no longer.

"How do I know? It must be Hebrew or Latin, or something. Hush!"

People at the front seemed to be chanting: "Pilate! Pilate!"

"What's that?" Veronica urged. "We didn't learn that, did we?"

Victor shot a look round. No one seemed to have heard his persistent wife. He scowled fiercely down to quieten her.

All of a sudden a great wave of sound rolled up towards them. It started from a few voices in front and then swept towards them in an immense heave of emotion.

"Barabbas! Barabbas!"

Veronica almost leapt in the air with relief.

"Barabbas… Barabbas!" she chorused ecstatically. Victor grinned all over his face and joined his wife in the cry.

"Barabbas!" he hollered as if his throat would burst. It was great to shout aloud unrestrainedly.

The noise echoed around and around the square before eventually, slowly, dying away. The crowd was now excitedly pressing forward and Victor and Veronica could see a little more clearly what was going on. On the balcony in front, beside the man in the Roman toga, were a number of soldiers, four or five others in long hooded robes and one skinny man, bearded, dressed in purple with what looked like a bramble bush in his hair. As this one was pushed forward towards them on the balcony, the crowd erupted. The noise was deafening. Shouts, screams and whistles rent the air. Arms and fists were waving everywhere. Immense waves of sound rolled back and forth, filling the square with thick emotion.

"Crucify him! Crucify him!"

The crowd were in one voice: faces everywhere were lit with passion and excitement.

"Crucify him!" The Vulturas were on their toes, shouting until they were hoarse.

The man in purple was taken away and all those on the balcony disappeared. Immediately the crowd turned and began dissolving in a mad rush to get away. People started running, scrambling to get back up the paths out of the city. Victor and Veronica were roughly thrust apart and both had to fight to prevent themselves from being trodden underfoot. The mob seemed to go crazy. People were kicking and punching each other in their desperation to get uphill as soon as possible. Those who had been at the back of the crowd in the square found now that they were in the lead on the way out of town and everyone behind was clawing to get past.

The mob streamed up the hillside. Hundreds and hundreds of people fought and struggled higher like ants in an ant-heap. Victor and Veronica, both lost and desperate, scrambled like everyone else in a panic not to go under. All sense of time and place had now disappeared in the madness; they were somewhere on a hillside in a boiling sea of humanity.

Moving relentlessly onward and upward, slowly the frenzy seemed to subside. The crowd at last began to settle into a rhythm and the air of quiet expectancy gradually returned. Clouds in the sky above grew thicker and darker as the day wore on and from everywhere around, from the city behind and the hills on either side, there came a slow spreading silence. No bird sang; there was not a breath of wind to stir the leaves. It seemed as if the whole world was waiting.

Somewhere in the middle of the ant-heap, Victor and

Veronica at last saw each other. Separated by some thirty people, their searching eyes met. Her clothes torn and dirty, hair covered in dust and eyes streaked with tears, Veronica jumped up in happiness and relief at the sight of her husband's worried face, looking for hers.

At that moment the lowering skies parted and a shaft of sunlight struck the hilltop. Three crosses were briefly illuminated, and were there not figures up there now, silhouetted against them? A huge cry went up from the assembly and people were on their feet again, shouting and chanting and waving their fists in the air.

Victor and Veronica rushed together, fearful of being separated again as the mood of excitement heightened. If this was History, they had had enough of it.

'Whizz-clunk!' It sounded as if someone was throwing stones. Now the Vulturas looked to get away; they stumbled downwards, clutching on to one another. 'Whizz-clunk!' Another stone? Victor declined to look but concentrated now on keeping upright and finding the way back to their time capsule below them. Clunk! Clunk! Clunk! A clattering shower fell behind them.

Other couples rose also and started to move away. Thankfully there was no frenzied rush this time. Instead the crowd slowly and steadily dissipated as people picked their way downhill and back to their homes. Victor and Veronica finally spotted their own destination and made their way towards it.

Veronica was bursting to speak: "Oh Victor, where did you get to? I nearly *died* losing you like that, wasn't it awful? I just couldn't keep up with everyone else in these crazy clothes."

Victor was about to reply when he stopped short, listening. Snatches of conversation from other couples drifted past. He shook his head in disbelief and walked on.

Whizz-clunk! Victor span around but saw nothing. Only a group of people who had stopped a little way away, one man seemingly clutching his stomach. He was fumbling with his clothes as he looked back up the hill.

Finally the Vulturas reached the Time Travel capsule. The other tourists were all there, waiting for them outside. Their marvellous machine was really wonderfully camouflaged, Veronica could not help remarking to her husband, like every other building around, except of course it contained all that wizard gadgetry.

Victor nodded slowly in agreement and wandered over to a nearby house to take a look and compare. Peeking into the gloomy interior of the other structure, on a blackened tabletop he could just make out the dimly glowing green announcement: "Euler's Ethnic Jump Jet. Leap right into another dimension!"

Victor stepped backwards and looked around as if in a daze. He saw people trickling back into the city from all over the hillside and finally he Understood.

"What's the problem, honey?" Veronica asked, seeing her husband's strange behaviour.

"All these people..." Victor hesitated. "Listen! Can't you hear?"

"Hear what?"

"What they're speaking! Listen... it... it's *English*! And look, that man over there with his hands in front of him – he's concealing a camera!"

Whizz-clunk! Another shutter clicked and another photograph was taken.

Veronica looked around and laughed. It was true. People were clustered in groups outside buildings all over Jerusalem: exactly as they were. Tourists all of them. She waved at one who had just finished eating and was throwing an empty yoghurt pot out of the window across the way.

"Hi there!" she giggled. "Great show, wasn't it?"

Victor hurriedly pushed his wife into their capsule, not noticing the dented Coca-Cola can he stumbled over.

"C'mon, let's get out of here!" he barked at the travel courier. "I've had enough of this place."

"Oh but, Victor, why all the rush now?" Veronica stalled. "Let's go out and meet people."

Her husband's face reddened. "Veronica, don't you understand? Don't you see what we've done?"

Mrs Veronica Vultura looked blank, uncomprehending.

"It was all of *us* out there. Our people from our Time. Back here in Jerusalem... and we did it... don't you see? *We* crucified Christ!"

END

The audience on the balcony applauded enthusiastically.

"Oh well done, sir!" cried Hernando. "An excellent illustration of the folly of modern society. We who are so proud, think we are so advanced, and yet we are condemned to repeat the mistakes of the past!"

"Historical analysis is a form of exploration, as you were discussing earlier," said Jeroen, "searching for evidence in past writings... but I confess the further I look, the more I see the same patterns I have seen before!"

"But is that really true?" said Hugo. "Do we never learn? Might it not be that you see our communal folly because that is what you expect to find?"

"Possibly... but in decades of study it is remarkable just how much folly I've seen!"

"A problem with all observation!" cried Ivan, the mathematician. "I struggle with that all the time in my research. We see what we best recognise and tend not to notice what is genuinely new."

"The same for myself," said Hugo. "All scientific progress begins with observation – like Newton seeing an apple fall and asking: why? Such insight leads to new hypotheses and then setting up experiments to test their implications. But none of that can begin without first objectively measuring what you observe. The problem is that it is so difficult not to let your own prejudices influence what you see."

"Mmmm," ruminated David. "A good scientist does not see what he wants to see when it isn't there and does see what he doesn't want to see when it is there!"

"Time for a story about that," said Hugo.

Chapter 6

Science: A Hitch in Time

It was a boot.

A standard, black, size ten Flexiplas boot – so ordinary and unremarkable an object that it would not normally draw anybody's attention to it.

Except that this boot came tumbling silently through space, slowly corkscrewing its way into radar range and it was now finally appearing on Oscar's video screen.

It was such a totally unexpected sight that Oscar was dumbstruck. He goggled at it disbelievingly. Maybe his instruments were locked into some sort of time loop and were displaying an earlier recording? This thing could not be *a boot*. Not out here!

He checked over the control panel. No. Nothing was out of order. The signal he was picking up was exactly as portrayed: a boot. It was identical to the sort of footwear sported by hundreds of navigators as they piloted their machines all over the known universe. Indeed, the one shown by his camera was so familiar that it might just as well be Oscar's own. He *had* to believe it.

But what really unsettled him was that Oscar knew he was further out in the galaxy than any person had ever been before. He was drawing a curve across the uncharted heavens, mapping the void several light months beyond the reach of any previous mortal, and yet here came this insolent black boot, spiralling towards him from the direction of deep space.

What was it doing here?

Oscar began feverishly gathering data. He first had to calculate the bearing and relative speed of the incoming missile. In order to do this he copied all the details of his ship's movements on to a new file and added to this the trajectory of the radar plots of the mystery newcomer. He was not mistaken. The boot was moving into inhabited space from out of the emptiness. Its velocity was a shock, however. By the time he had manoeuvred alongside and closed within an arm's length of it he found he was accelerating towards the Solar System at close to light speed. He was arching back to where he had come from at a rate faster than he had originally set out.

This was baffling. Where had the boot come from? For how long had it been spinning in on its lonely orbit from nowhere? Oscar pored over the bank of instrumentation in front of him and quickly finished off all possible examination of this uninvited piece of interstellar flotsam. The forest of antennae pinned to the outside of his craft could do no more. The vacuum of space prevented him from getting his hands on the boot but his cramped surveyship was equipped with a robot maintenance bug which Oscar now sent out on a towline to capture his trophy. Once successfully stowed in the tiny cargo hold he could safely decelerate and then give himself enough time to figure out his next move. His pride would not allow him to leave the conundrum unsolved.

What is it about humankind that drives individuals to search far beyond the reaches of the known world? What is it that makes those like Columbus and Magellan risk all to follow some crazy scientific dream such as circumnavigation?

Ignorance kindled by imagination, perhaps? Certainly something more than mere self-interest: those solely concerned with their own welfare would surely find less risky ways to enrich themselves.

It can only be belief in something grander than one's self, allied (rightly or wrongly) to faith in the current state of science that tempts adventurers to sail out far from the safety of charted waters. Certainly Columbus was not to know when he set out with three small ships that his expedition across the Atlantic did not possess the technology to successfully circle the globe. The unknown world was far greater and more complex than ever he could have imagined at the time. But, in spite of his ignorance Columbus met with success and his achievement – although not what he intended – was, in time, to change the history of planet Earth.

Such deeds can provide inspiration for others to follow – though the dangers of such enterprise must never be underestimated. We are so small beneath the stars that the state of our ignorance can be immense. Where imagination fails the alien, unknown world begins. To venture here means to go beyond the limits of science, where only courage and good fortune can help.

Not that Oscar Zimmerman was now thinking much about these things. Coming in from the far horizons of interstellar space, his brain was struggling to re-emerge from its drugged state of time-slip. His consciousness seemed to swim and cannon around inside his skull until finally he regained full control of his senses. He forced his eyes to take a look outside the observation port. Yes! The heavens were reassuringly aligned in their classical constellations: He was back in the Solar time zone.

Oscar breathed deeply. He relaxed. Bringing his ship down within range of its homeport was a difficult business and he must have felt like the earliest navigators on reaching landfall – mightily relieved that he was back in recognisable waters again with all perils now behind him.

As he breathed out and his pulse eased, the reaction set in: there was all of thronging humanity out there. Oscar groaned. From one end of the Solar System to the other there was every sort of idiot zipping about, chasing their tiny-minded lives, insisting on compliance with damn-fool regulations that serve no purpose; either that or someone somewhere was always trying to trick you out of your money in the seconds you paused to scratch your head. He hated society! For Oscar, anywhere within light hours of the Sun was overcrowded.

Oscar panned his communications systems around to pick up the nearest outstation. The signal came through loud and clear:

"Sector Delta Red. This is Station Spinoza. We see you: Triple F surveyship No. 703. Welcome back to Earth time!"

Oscar grunted to himself in recognition of the message. Station Spinoza was probably the largest and undoubtedly the most popular of the number of communications and service stations that carved an ellipse around the Sun. It was a huge, independent enterprise, artlessly constructed, that cartwheeled slowly out beyond Pluto. It provided a rich and comprehensive array of passenger services and company hospitality to any and all returning starships that anchored within range. Oscar hated the place, of course, but he was nonetheless required to check in his corporation report and – he grudgingly admitted – despite its constant traffic of humanity, Station Spinoza was unfailingly efficient and his turn-round time here was probably shorter than at any other port of call.

Oscar locked on to Spinoza's homing beacon, turned down his nuclear drive and then stretched back and closed his eyes. It was all over now: no more navigating the dangers of the deep; no more heart-thumping risks or brain draining time-slips. His small, one-man surveyship would be brought automatically in to its destination, its powerful engines shut off and the ship moored wherever the station's duty officer thought most appropriate.

Spinoza's entertainment guide hijacked Oscar's communication system. Samples of modern and classical music assaulted his ears and eyes, also a variety of different dramatic offerings. He pulsed through them all to pause for a moment over the news and information band. Independent stations were always worth listening to more than the others – if any were worth it at all.

Things had not changed much: Gemini and Triple F were still making extravagant claims for themselves as always; squabbling continued amongst the minor corporations and the odd death and disaster was being relayed back from less developed, less important time zones. At the moment it was kidnapping and piracy in Epsilon Tauri. As if anyone really cared about that part of the Galaxy.

Oscar tuned into the domestic services broadcast. The hologram in his small cabin whizzed through scores of allegedly fascinating, not-to-be-missed bargains available on-station. From bars to bar mitzvahs, saunas to stock markets, it was difficult for Oscar to take it all in. He shook his head as if this could help him understand the strange language. Back from prospecting a solitary path through the furthest stars accessible to man and the Triple F Corporation, he was more out of his depth here – where the whole environment was designed to cater for every human need – than parsecs away in a truly alien environment.

Angry and impatient with this irrelevant junk, Oscar deleted all such incoming signals from contaminating his receivers. He tuned in then to see what services Triple F offered to its personnel at this site. This looked more encouraging: a long list of facilities. Oscar was particularly interested to see if they had anything much in the way of research laboratories on board, or whether he had to wait until he got back to a Triple F base station proper. He was in luck: a small laboratory was located in the heart of the corporation's terminal, staffed by a Dr Konstantin Romanov.

"Come in, Mr Zimmerman, sir. Welcome to Triple F, Spinoza." The bright-eyed receptionist punched in the admission key and stood up to greet him.

Oscar grunted. "This branch has grown since I was here last. Where do I go?"

"Follow straight through, sir. We picked up your signal some time ago, so if you go into the pink area here you'll find we are all ready for you."

Oscar nodded his approval and moved past. It was an impressive layout of offices and luxury lounges that met his eyes. A large FFF in three pastel shades was picked out in the soft, heavy pile carpet that cushioned his feet. Nothing had been spared to impress the casual visitor. On the edge of the Solar System, where constructing and maintaining life support systems in zero gravity costs billions of credits for every cubic metre, the sweet tasting air, the Earth-like gravity and the sheer volume of uncrowded recreational space that stretched out in front of him spoke volumes about Triple F's economic power. The corporation's Spinoza terminal spread out in three directions to fill an entire outer segment of the giant space station.

The security clearance pink area was right in front of him. He checked in his identikey at the first booth and watched the barely visible security screen slide down behind him. A touch on the sensor plate and he was through to Mining Division.

"Hello, Oscar, you old ghost. We thought you were lost. You haven't been seen around in space for months! Anything new for us?"

Oscar snorted angrily in reply. The greeting was too hearty and over-familiar.

Elizabeth McCarthy, Triple F's on-station mining director, laughed. "The distant suns haven't improved your temper any! No luck again? More methane clouds and frozen storms?"

Oscar dumped his assorted discs, files and microfiches on to the desk in front of him. A larger vacuum case he kept at his side. "Instead of making wisecracks, try processing all this data and you can see what I've got for you. A planet or two that might yield something useful but with the lousy equipment you give me it's a wonder I've found anything. Get me a pass through to Dr Romanov in research and I'll let you know if there's anything more. And what about some thanks for doing the dirty work for this organisation? I'm still on the payroll am I, or have Triple F forgotten who finds their bread?"

Liz McCarthy's eyes swivelled upwards. It was no use trying to lighten up old Oscar Zimmerman.

"Your salary has been paid in as always, Oscar. Don't worry, you're fully appreciated. As regards research, seeing as it's you, I'll get clearance – just give me a minute." She logged in one of the discs piled in front of her. "Someone will get working on this lot right away. Come back later after you've taken a rest if you want to check the results." A series of unrecognisable patterns stared up at her from her VDU. She shrugged and cajoled the computer into more exercise. "Cross any other ships going your way?" she questioned.

"One of the independents was footling about close to my second light jump in Andromeda 15. Spacetug of Castlestone Company. Neat. Joel Turner's crew, I guess. He always has impressive outfits." Oscar couldn't resist the dig.

"Castlestone, eh? They show up in all sorts of unlikely time zones. You mind they're not following your star trails, Oscar. Especially Turner, he's good."

"Huh!" Oscar's hackles rose at the insinuation that others could follow anywhere close to him. "No one'll ever find anything worth claiming in my space. They don't have the stamina!"

He would never admit it but despite all his light-jump experience he knew there were probably as good navigators around as he, Turner amongst them. None however, he was sure, had the perseverance and determination to go further and search for longer in the Galaxy's limits. Oscar revelled in solitary, long-distance surveys far beyond the reach of normal space traffic and he knew he could take the physical and psychological discomfort longer than anyone.

Elizabeth McCarthy accepted the reassurance. "OK, take it easy, old scout. We're not too worried about the competition in your case. You're pretty unique, Oscar. No, we've got more problems closer in. I hear on some of the developing planets it's getting pretty close to naked aggression. Know anything?"

"Nope!" Oscar was anxious to go. He had absolutely no interest in whatever madness other people were up to elsewhere.

"C'mon – got my research pass yet?"

The console in front of Liz McCarthy blinked green. She looked up and smiled a goodbye: "Right! Off you go, Oscar, you're clear all the way through – just follow the yellow illuminated pathway. "

Little yellow lights every few paces led Oscar through a number of offices, on to a long passageway and through several security screens until he finally reached swing doors on his left marked: "Research Labs". On entry, he found a stocky, serious-looking individual in dark green Corporation uniform waiting for him. Purple flashes above the breast pocket indicated that this man was a senior assistant in the Research Department. He escorted Oscar into what looked like a boardroom – a number of executive armchairs around an oval table – and indicated that he should sit and wait.

A moment later a door opened on the other side and another uniform entered with the name *Dr Konstantin Romanov* embellished on it in purple letters. This man was the Head of the Department and he was all smiles and politeness. Oscar grunted: his visitor looked younger and less experienced than he liked. He guessed that this scientist was probably a recent, still-wet-behind-the-ears, postgrad product from Triple F's Institute of Technology – now farmed out to one of the less important stations where he could make mistakes where it did not matter.

Romanov beamed: "Dr Zimmerman, I am so pleased to make your acquaintance. I have heard so much about you. What can I do to help?"

Oscar banged down his case on to the table in front of him and snorted: "Be extremely careful with this! Make sure that there is *no possibility* of contamination before you open it up. I want to know exactly for how long it has been frozen. Geddit? *Exactly*. Down to the nearest millisecond. *If* you can do such measurements, that is. There's a timer enclosed since I first picked this up, subtract that time from the total you come up with and that'll give us an estimate of how long it has been out in space. The more accurate your estimate, the more precise I can be to its original location in the void. Of course, if you can't guarantee that you can do it accurately enough, then don't open it and I'll go somewhere else..."

Romanov's face didn't flicker. If he felt insulted, he did not show it. He leaned forward slightly and in a flat voice replied: "The operation is relatively simple, Dr Zimmerman. Given your clearance code, we can start on zis investigation almost immediately. As a result, you should have your answer within a couple of Earth hours. One moment..." The scientist took the case, stood up and called a colleague from the doorway. He turned and smiled again at his visitor: "Please excuse me, I shall be back in a second." He went out, closing the door behind him.

Oscar scowled his dissatisfaction. He was not one for social niceties, so maybe he had been a little harsh in his treatment of this research fellow, but a correct answer was vitally important to him. Couldn't such people understand? His fingers drummed on the table, signalling his impatience.

Romanov returned, easing himself into the chair opposite Oscar: "As I said, Dr Zimmerman, zis little job you have given us should not take too long. The laws of science and ze resources of Triple F are a very productive partnership, don't you agree?"

This smiling young man was altogether too polite and self-assured for someone as cantankerous and star weary as Oscar Zimmerman to stomach. He exploded:

"Laws of science? The laws of science are bullshit! We use them out in the middle of nowhere cos that's all we've got to go on – but you've gotta interpret them with a very healthy dose of scepticism. *Nothing* is certain!"

"Oh but they are, Dr Zimmerman! You can bet your life on ze laws of science! That is what you are doing all the time, isn't it? I'm told you are the Corporation's most travelled navigator and so do you not fly from one end of the Galaxy to ze other thanks to the predictability and reliability of physical laws? If such laws were not so literally universal you could not come back and be discussing zis here with me now!" He possessed the patient insistence of someone well versed in his trade.

"Listen! We all use these so-called laws of science in order to make some sense of the chaos that surrounds us. I wanna have a few clues to help me fathom the black infinity... that's what I'm waiting here for: for you to give me my next lead. But I don't fool myself that all that is out there adds up to some coherent whole. People have been tricked into believing that since they first left the trees on Earth. Don't tell me you're another one still looking for the Holy Grail! It's an illusion."

Dr Konstantin Romanov stopped smiling and for a moment his face took on a very solemn air: "Dr Zimmerman, current research in cosmology and in quantum mechanics is on the verge of producing a complete unified theory zat is capable of describing and accounting for everything in ze universe. I can assure you..."

"Pah!" Another explosive retort cut him short. "Hawking was saying that at the end of the twentieth century! Look how far that got him! Almost as soon as he said it they started finding anomalies all over the place. Now we take some laws for granted – dammit I hitch rides on them across the Galaxy – but you guys still can't quite explain how and why I can do it. That's cos your famous laws keep changing. You are rewriting them all the time. They're not infallible laws of science – they're the laws of fallible man."

Romanov's smile returned: "There is some truth in saying zat we are rewriting, or rather refining, our laws... *the* laws of science... but zey are not so fickle and unreliable as humankind – as you imply. The reason you can hitch a ride around an anomaly *is* explainable in ze curvature of space-time – and just as well that we *can* explain it, my dear sir, or you wouldn't try it!"

Oscar Zimmerman really lost his cool now. He leapt up: "Don't you start telling me what I would or would not try! Out there at the other end of a light slip it's not your precious laws of science that *I* rely on. Godammit!! I know only too well that you guys have just *dreamt up* the latest law. Your biggest worry is whether or not some other damn fool sitting in a committee somewhere will or will not accept it for publication. Big deal! I bet there are scores of scientists really shittin' themselves over their latest pet theory. Meanwhile I'm out there on the edge of an anomaly about to press a button and wondering if I'll end up strung out like spaghetti! You should try it, sunshine! It gives you a whole new outlook on scientific experimentation when it is *you* that's the guinea pig."

"Please, Dr Zimmerman! Do not take offence!" Romanov did his best to placate his volatile guest. "I do not wish in any way to denigrate ze extremely courageous and valuable work you are doing for the Corporation and for our understanding of ze universe. You are quite right. We are all humble pencil pushers locked away here compared to your valiant exploits in surveying ze galactic highways. I only wish to reassure you that each and every discovery you make is helping us in the progress of science. Every step you make leads us a little closer to understanding ze underlying order in the universe…"

Oscar sat back down with a bang and glared at his companion: "There is *no underlying order*, you dummy! It's all illusion; smoke-screen; stardust. There's nothing but chaos out there! The patterns you see are not *out there* waiting to be discovered – they're in your head. Look: ever since Galileo you astronomers said there were canals on Mars. Three hundred years later you changed your tune – it wasn't water in them, but lichen. But they were still canals – lines you thought you saw on the red dust. Of course! You had no other concepts to describe them. For close on 400 years you thought you saw canals – right up until the mid-twentieth century when better telescopes at last showed them to be figments of imagination: observers had extrapolated patterns in the chaos. Don't you see: humans have an insatiable *need* to see order, to make sense of it all." He threw his hands up in despair.

"People have been seeing things out there since the beginning of time. First it was a flat Earth with the sun and stars revolving around it. Then it was a sun-centred system with damn fool Martian canals. Then it was an expanding universe but light speed was the absolute limit. Now we have a stable universe yet a curved sense of space-time with no limits. All these 'truths' are getting more and more short-lived: what you don't realise is that they're *all* bullshit. Pure invention. Bah! You youngsters have no appreciation of how fallible we are!"

Patronised and insulted, Dr Konstantin Romanov nonetheless tried gently to calm down his guest and turn the discussion to an area where they could both agree. "Like you say, Dr Zimmerman, we are all trying to make sense of ze chaos, to make predictions which we can test to corroborate our theories. We are testing something for you right now, yes? What do you hope it will show us?"

"Hummmph!" Oscar snorted again. All his natural instincts were to keep things close to his chest – especially when confronted by those he had little respect for. The trouble was, he had next to no respect for *anyone*. And the fact was that he actually needed this department's co-operation – especially if, as he guessed, he was going to have to ask for more of Triple F's indulgence to go chasing after what was in effect a scientific curiosity. Any economic rewards were likely to be very long term, if any.

"I dunno... it could be nothing... it could be something of immense importance..." He screwed up his eyes and squinted at the questioning face of the other. He snorted once more. If anything, Dr Konstantin Romanov possessed an open, even naïve expression. He did not look like one of those cynical, too-clever-by-half types likely to laugh at him behind his back as soon as he had left. Oscar decided to risk it:

"That boot came out of nowhere. The record of its trajectory I've not released yet..." He tapped his pocket where he had retained the crucial memory disc. "But I need your help to confirm its precise origins. If the latest Triple F reports are to be relied upon, no other manned craft has been out that way – only a Gemini auto-probe several light hours distant and going on a completely different bearing. But this boot has obviously been jettisoned from some inhabited site, so what explains it?

"There are two possibilities. One is that Triple F and Gemini are locked into such a fierce, if not downright militaristic competition that they are concealing their movements not only to each other but also within their own organisations. That is a distinct possibility. It wouldn't be the first time that somebody was shooting at somebody else somewhere and denying it all. But even if this *is* the case, I don't think I would have missed seeing some movement in the outer limits where I've been. Nobody knows *that* distant star sector better than I.

"The other possibility is that there is an uncharted anomaly out there which is doing something really weird. That boot *cannot* have come from somewhere beyond the reach of humankind. But the only explanation that leaves is that it must have blinked out of existence somewhere nearer the Solar System going in one direction, circumnavigated the Galaxy and then reappeared to come rifling back at me on an entirely different track. How is that possible? Was it swallowed up in one anomaly to be spat out from another? Traversing across the stars in the twinkling of an eye? See what I mean? It challenges all known theories of space and time... not that I have much faith in any of *that*..."

Romanov nodded. "This is very interesting, Dr Zimmerman. You will have our results in just a few moments now when my assistant returns. But you intend to go back there do you not? When you have a better idea as to exactly where zis item originated? Yes? Then you must take more measurements of any gravity changes in this region; also ze emission of gamma rays, temperature, well just about everything. I am sure you know…"

"You're darn right. I'm not going to go charging around anywhere near there without a much clearer picture of where any event horizon might lie. This is not the first time I've been plumbing the depths of our collective ignorance. But I've got this gut feeling that all notions of space-time break down there… maybe I'll go racing off into the future somehow… I don't know…" He quietened down into pensive introspection.

Konstantin Romanov took advantage of this hiatus in the conversation to rise quietly and leave the room. With his explosive and unpredictable visitor now in a more contemplative frame of mind this was the moment to go and see if the results were ready. But Romanov was nervous. He was hoping that there would be no more surprises waiting that would provoke further outbursts.

Elizabeth McCarthy's beeper sounded and she turned to switch through the call.

"Hello, Elizabeth!" It was Romanov's face that came into focus. "He's on his way back to you now."

"How did you get on?"

"Well I must thank you for ze warning – I was as polite and welcoming as possible, but that still did not prevent fireworks. Just as you said: he really is ze most difficult of customers!"

Triple F's on-station Mining Director laughed. "Well congratulations for surviving, Konstantin! There are very few people who can bear him for long and I guessed in your case you'd have trouble. My heart sank when I heard him ask for you. But did you manage to get him what he wanted?"

"Yes. All details are on ze net so you've got a full record of the investigation we carried out. But I've got to brief you fully before he gets to you. Can you stall him outside when he arrives?"

Looking away, Elizabeth closed down the screens around her

office and warned her secretary to keep all callers at bay. Then she turned her full attention back to the VDU once more.

"OK, Konstantin. Go ahead."

"I'll spare you the details of the argument we had – suffice to say he insulted me, my profession and everyone else he could think of since Galileo. He actually came to ask for a de-con report on zis *boot* he brought in – of all crazy things. Said he found it coming through space at him on his last trip, way out on the edge of the Galaxy. Given the data we've found, he says he will be able to identify its precise origins and zat is where he will be heading next.

"Well he has got what he wanted – ze boot had been frozen for sixteen days, seven hours, twenty-three minutes and eleven point three eight seconds before he picked it up. All the details are there for you on file. According to his story, zat puts the boot's origins someway out in sterile space where – he says – he will want to go chasing right away. If he does so, I guess zat is good for Triple F – in that it keeps him away from some sensitive areas right now – though you'd be a better judge of that than me.

"But get this – when he told me how he had first picked this boot up I thought: zis does not sound right! No sir! He's flying out on the edge of the spiral arm with emptiness for light years all around, but he picks up zis tiny, unique piece of interstellar flotsam apparently only two weeks after it has come into existence. The odds on this happening are billions to one against! And *how* does it come into existence? Some anomaly has given *birth* to it! Is he crazy or something? Or maybe he thinks I am crazy and will swallow his story? Zis is another insult for me!

"But I don't want trouble with zis crazy man. No thank you! So before he gets his boot back I ask my department to get as much information about it as possible – I do not trust his story, you see. We do a DNA search on whatever evidence we can find inside this boot. There are bound to be traces of human sweat, you see. Success! We find enough to serve our investigation. Then we try to match what we've got with what we can find on all the DNA files we have access to. We try records of personnel for all people zat I have clearance for: in Gemini, in the independents, for all navigators or passengers that might possibly be out there. We try Triple F last of all – because I am thinking that Dr Zimmerman would be sure to know if any other Triple F ship had been out his way. I should have tried zese records first of all and saved a lot of bother! Why? Because we get a perfect DNA match. The boot belongs to no one else other than the very crazy Dr Oscar Zimmerman!"

"What... what are you telling me?" Liz McCarthy was having trouble following this strange story.

"Dr Zimmerman says he has found something that challenges all ze laws of science. He will be coming to you soon – I am sure – insisting on a full expeditionary survey of a sector in space zat only he knows of. This expedition, he will claim, is of supreme scientific importance. But ze evidence his claim is built on he invented himself!! I am sure he simply heaved his own boot out into space for sixteen days so as to give himself something to show us, to support his story."

"But... but... hold on, Konstantin! Why would he want to equip a major expedition as you say?" Elizabeth was still struggling to come to terms with all this.

"I don' know! Your knowledge of him is better than mine. Maybe he wants to poke his nose in somewhere uninvited?

"Mmmm. Thank you, Konstantin." Elizabeth needed to think. "I take it you're sure of this DNA match? That this boot really *is* Oscar's? And does he know you have found this out?"

"Please, Elizabeth! Do not start insulting my work also! Of course I am sure... and no, Dr Zimmerman knows nothing of all this zat I am telling you."

Elizabeth McCarthy sighed. Poor Konstantin was clearly feeling bruised by his encounter with Triple F's most idiosyncratic navigator. All these sensitive men! She thanked him again and reassured him that his opinion was respected. His scientific thoroughness was indeed recognised, which was why Triple F had appointed him to such an important post. As a judge of character, however, Romanov's touch was less certain. The insinuation that Oscar might want to go poking around in sensitive time zones where Gemini and Triple F were in dispute she was sure was wrong. Oscar had absolutely no patience for such rivalries. Nor, she guessed, was he capable of such Machiavellian manoeuvring as the suggestion that he had fabricated evidence implied. But then what *was* he up to?

It was probably best to ask Oscar directly. Elizabeth raised the security screens and informed her secretary that she was now ready to receive incoming calls.

It was not long before the subject of her speculation arrived. Oscar Zimmerman came bustling in, plumped himself down and, in his usual brusque fashion, demanded to know if all the information he had brought back had been processed already.

This gave Elizabeth her chance:

"Well I've fed through to Head Office all your data, but look here, Oscar: Have you been holding out on us? There was no log of the last day of your ship's movements before we find you reversing engines and making tracks to come here. Now why is that?"

Oscar's temperature immediately started to rise. He went red faced and started twisting in his chair. "Why don't people in this space station start talking to each other? Then you would already know! Try contacting that young imbecile you have in research if you want to find out."

"Now come on, Oscar, suppose you tell me. Konstantin's report will already be filed, I am sure – he is a very efficient operator. But I'd much prefer to hear it from you. Plus you have to check in all your movements anyway – you know the regulations."

"Regulations, regulations, regulations! Don't you people think

of anything else? I'm sick to death of your stupid regulations..."
He was just about to set off into another flight of invective but
Elizabeth was having none of it.

"Oh come off it, Oscar! You know you are going to have to tell
me anyway so stop stalling! What have you found?"

The twisting and turning in his chair continued. Oscar hated
being forced out into the open. He was not ready yet to give up
all his information, not until after he had had the chance to go
out and do a little more digging. He had to release to the
Research Department the evidence he had found in order to get
a lead on where to search next – but he jealously wanted to guard
the precise location to himself. If he released the bearing of his
ship's last movements that would reveal all.

The struggle on his face was all too obvious. Elizabeth smiled.
She was more certain than ever that this peppery, quarrelsome
individual was essentially harmless. Poor Oscar! He needed
protection from himself!

"Time travel!" he finally blurted out. "That's what it might be!
Damn scientists don't have enough imagination to figure it out,
but if you come across something that has no right to be there, it
can only be because it travelled halfway across the Galaxy in the
blink of an eyelash."

He was staring so intently, so stubbornly in front of him that
Elizabeth knew he was telling the truth. He was so transparent
that there was not the faintest possibility that he was capable of
any political game playing.

"Oh, Oscar! Are you sure? It sounds... pretty... er...
unusual..." Elizabeth did not want to sound too discouraging for
fear of setting him off again.

"No I'm *not* sure!" Oscar retorted hotly. "I'm not sure of
anything except that Triple F has got to send me out there again
so that I can check it out. I don't want any other damn fools
blasting their trails around there and fouling up the ether.
Geddit? I don't want anyone or anything anywhere near until

I've finished surveying that sector. Can you get me that clearance? And do you think you can keep it quiet?" He turned to glare aggressively at Triple F's senior representative at Spinoza: she was the one with the authority to decide.

Elizabeth sighed once more. What a mess these men were giving her! She was sure Oscar genuinely believed that he was on to something important. But if Romanov's report was correct, apparently Oscar was not aware of the true nature of his find. That meant he was all set to go off on a wild goose chase! The Corporation could not afford to so obviously waste resources like that.

"Oscar... what you found... you couldn't have accidentally jettisoned it yourself could you?" She said it as gently as she could.

Oscar exploded. "What do you take me for? Some wet-behind-the ears surveyor fresh from college? I can't do my job if any of my readings are contaminated. If only other navigators were as careful as me there wouldn't be nearly so much junk out there in space. When I'm surveying I barely discharge *any* energy – yet I half expect to get blown in two by discarded Coke cans whenever I get within days of the Solar System! Take it from me: there is no one out there who leaves less of a trail between the stars than I do!"

"OK, OK, OK, take it easy!" Elizabeth cut him short again. "Now listen to this: it's Triple F's resources you're burning up. I know you don't like it, Oscar, but that means you've got to play it by the book. You are the one who always wants to go further and further into deep space but you've got to realise that every time you go out into even more remote areas, the lower the probability there is of you ever earning us sufficient returns. You know it's true. You said yourself that there's not much of economic value in your current survey report but at the same time you're asking to go back and go even further into the void on the basis of just one piece of anomalous evidence. We can't afford to keep on funding your wild goose chases!"

She held up her hand to try and stop him from rising out of his chair: "Now don't go losing your temper on me. I'm only giving you the picture as the Corporation sees it. OK? Sure, there is always the possibility that on your very next tour you'll hit pay dirt and pay us back in spades... but you've been spinning that line in just about every Triple F office in the Galaxy for years, so far as I understand it. It can't go on like this...

"Look – I want to help you if I can, alright? Let's do it this way: First, give me your last log that you're holding back on. You've gotta do that. I cannot let you go out again without a full report on your latest movements. It's more than my job's worth to let you take that risk. Don't worry about anyone else wanting to go out that way after you. They won't! Second, if you *must* spend months out doing your own thing, make sure that on your way you get a complete record of *every* lump of rock or passing starship that comes into range. That way, I can just about defend this last shot in the darkness. You're a surveyor. That's what you'll be doing: Head Office can't complain too much. As regards chasing bits of flotsam into nowhere – that'll win you no friends at all but if you're out there we can't really stop you. Though get this – if you come back with nothing worth developing this time don't expect that the Corporation will be interested in funding any more of your long shots in the future... This is your last chance, understand?"

Oscar Zimmerman, Triple F's most travelled navigator, stormed back to his surveyship more foul tempered than ever. His fierce glowering and snorts of rage distanced himself from all other space crew waiting in Spinoza's shuttle bug. Time could not go fast enough in this overpopulated place: he couldn't wait to strap himself in front of his own controls and gain clearance to take the fastest route out, space-side.

As soon as he had clambered aboard and switched on, he

thumped the nuclear drive on to full thrust – even though he knew that Spinoza's override would prevent his ship from radiating too much energy until he was well out of the station's orbit. Banging the controls around in his own spacecraft did not achieve much, but it helped a little. Oscar loaded the most mind-blanking music into his sound system and pulsed up the volume. He started shouting out the instrument readings into the closed space also. It all helped a little more.

"Stardrive, stardrive... now! Zero one... come on, come on! Zero two... zero four... zero seven... Yes!" He keyed in the coordinates for his next destination. "Two thousand... six thousand... uuuugh!"

Powerful motors roaring way back behind him pushed Oscar deep into his control couch as if the world he was leaving was hanging on desperately and did not want to let him go. Inside the cockpit, as his mind began to swim, music blared and the head-up display unit blurred with numbers that changed in colour from blue to red to yellow. Thunderous acceleration shook everything. The lonely spacecraft soared into the heavens, its nuclear drive a tiny bead of starlight all to itself in the deepening blackness. It twinkled; it shimmered and then suddenly, as if switched off, it was gone.

To all observers in the Earth time zone, Oscar Zimmerman now no longer existed. His spacecraft had simply disappeared and no known tracking system could find him.

Rushing headlong towards an event horizon, at a certain rate of acceleration and on a given bearing, time begins to slip... as do all previously known notions of light, energy and space. On fairly well established trade routes now, all the critical coordinates were well charted and countless spacecraft had frozen time as they skidded around the edges of black holes in the Galaxy. They were thus able to jump across space far more quickly than had been thought possible, unhitching their ride to come out into an entirely new time zone, constellations ahead of where they had started.

Away from the proven trade routes, however, things were more difficult. The problem was that even after centuries of research, time was still a great, big, black box of a subject. It wandered in places pattern-less across the universe. Anomalies existed. Time-slip speed near one location was sometimes unpredictably different to that near another. Hitting an event horizon at one point in space-time could spin a ship out somewhere totally unexpected. It was like those ancient mariners sailing into a hurricane that would blow their ship out of control for days and sink all their instruments. Some navigators never came back. How could they? They did not know where they were and could set no coordinates for the return journey. They would search for eternity in uncharted parts of the Galaxy, with no recognised star patterns to guide them, light-years adrift and emitting signals that would never reach anyone in time. Some – who knows – may even have jumped clean out into the intergalactic void with screaming black space all around them, eyes and instruments searching hopelessly, ever more insanely, for any distant light or radar source that looked remotely familiar. Navigation was thus not riskless. Even on the more populous routes, the dark, bottomless possibilities of time-slip error gnawed at the mind. Ferdinand Magellan: your brothers and sisters suffer still.

After a predetermined interval, retro-rockets fired into life, slamming Oscar back into consciousness. Downside of the time-slip, he suddenly materialised within the reach of a brilliant, drenching sun.

It was Theta Andromeda: host to a widely spread, twenty-two planet solar system that had everything from heaving giants ten times the size of Jupiter down to spinning lumps of chewing gum with no constant shape or orbit.

"Red alert! Red alert! You are converging on to our flight

path!" Clarion voices blared at Oscar, warning him to steer clear.

Muttering obscenities, Oscar switched quickly into short-range radar steering and felt his surveyship pull round automatically to starboard. Sunlight and shadow played patterns through the observation port as he continued deceleration on a new tack.

"What in damnation is that thing doing here?" Oscar swore out loud as his camera panned round to reveal an enormous space train floating past. It was a fourteen-segment caterpillar with the words *General Mining Inc.* stencilled in huge letters along its length, sluggishly powering its way out towards oblivion. The mighty spaceship would probably take several Earth weeks before it built up enough push to escape Theta's time zone.

Oscar tuned into the inter-ship radio frequency and poured invective into the microphone: "Are you trying to wipe out all incoming space traffic or something? Go and wave that overgrown baseball bat somewhere else in the Galaxy!"

The giant Gemini spacecraft ignored his call. It slid past, one segment slowly after the other, shunting its massive load of mineral supplies across the heavens. The occupied control centre up front, dwarfed in relation to the rest of the vessel, remained silent and steady on its Earth-bound course.

Fuming at his neighbour's regal indifference, Oscar's unplanned evasive action now gave him a problem of reprogramming his own route. He pulsed a whole new set of questions into his control console, grateful that amongst the new equipment he had managed to browbeat out of Spinoza was included the latest navigational software.

His surveyship banked once more, giving Oscar another chance to view the slow-moving star monster.

"Big!" he thought. "The biggest I've seen." He wondered where it had come from. Probably one of the inner planets where mineral resources were more accessible than farther out. His eyes followed the giant ore containers, each one linked to the next in a long line in front of their straining nuclear locomotive.

"Christ knows how much they've got wrapped up in there… enough rock to create a new moon!"

Mindful of Elizabeth McCarthy's injunction to record all phenomena that he came in range of, Oscar switched on his battery of data-gathering equipment. At the same time he began to consider the implications of what he could see passing by in front of him. The sheer size of the space train spoke eloquently about the scale and complexity of the operations that must have created such a monster. There must firstly be an extensive system of mines somewhere, carving great slices out of a planet. It would have to be a minor planet with low gravity because a huge launch pad facility would be needed to lift off the mountains of ore extracted, as well as bring down all the heavy mining equipment required. All that would mean a sophisticated settlement dome almost certainly existed on the planet, probably with back-up systems in a lunar orbiting station. Finally, above the planet also there would have to be a fleet of donkey ships to receive the cargo and knock it into line. They would weld the entire structure together, ready to receive the incoming locomotive. All this was then inevitably destined for one of Gemini's giant factory stations circling Earth.

"Gemini's shifting a lot of rock," he spoke into his memory file. "They have an Earth-bound train bigger than anything I've ever seen coming out of Theta Andromeda before. Are you guys up with them here?"

The Theta Andromeda system was relatively recently developed and Oscar guessed – if things were going according to precedent – that the two big corporations of Gemini and Triple F were racing each other to get settlements established on top of the easiest recoverable reserves. Gemini was obviously well into production on at least one planet so far as he could see but, never bothering with his own corporation's downline reports, he had no idea if Triple F were anywhere in the running.

Oscar switched over to his medium-range radar scanner. As

his surveyship moved ahead further on his own interplanetary route he began casting round to see if he could pick up any other spacecraft. He ought to be able to check on a number of probable developments: as well as the big Gemini-Triple F duopoly, the minor corporations could be expected to be sniffing around to pick up anything their bigger brethren had missed. A variety of independent prospecting, construction, haulage or service companies might also be buzzing around somewhere – especially if there were rich reserves available and the two big empires had trouble getting enough hardware on site in time.

Nothing showed up around the closest planet to him: Theta Andromeda 6. Oscar had come out of the trade route time-slip relatively close to the host sun so only a few of the inner planets would be within range of his scanner at a resolution detailed enough to pick up spacecraft movement. Theta Andromeda 4 would be within reach soon, Theta 5 being on the far side of its orbit.

Time passed and nothing showed. It was a matter of great good fortune that Oscar had emerged on the interstellar highway in this time zone at the precise moment that he was within sight of another spacecraft. Now it seemed that there was nothing else at all in the heavens – though he had already deduced that that could not be true.

As if to confirm this, the radar screen began to bleep. And bleep again. Suddenly it was screeching electronically in panic. Whatever the radar scanner was picking up, it was closing at a speed so fast as to trigger all the alarm circuits.

For the second time, Oscar switched into emergency short-range radar steering and hunched down into the control couch to wait out the impending shock.

Nothing happened. With his eyes glued to the screen, Oscar watched something come firing into range, quickly decelerate and then veer away. Whatever it was, it had decided to leave him alone.

"Wheeee!" Oscar whistled in anticlimax. He switched all his instrumentation into short range to see if he could identify his mystery visitor.

He just caught the outline of something beetling away as fast as it came in. In a second it had faded, leaving no call sign, no video record and with the inter-ship radio frequency buzzing back at him unhelpfully. Who or whatever was out there was transmitting nothing but static. Oscar was reduced to guesswork.

"Well *that* will need checking against data you've got on foreign spacecraft." Oscar was speaking to the Triple F executive who would one day be examining this recording. "See if Gemini have got anything that conforms to the trajectory I've captured there. My guess is they've got an escort for their space train. Maybe some sort of security patrol? A gunship? Whatever it is, it's jamming most of my receivers."

Oscar thought about this: "Any reason they're nervous about me? Why have I been checked over? Should I have been briefed about this sector's activity?"

Oscar switched off the recorder and started cursing again. "Mining Division know I'm coming this way so if there's any trouble out here they should have let me know. I can't be expected to scan through all the company reports – why the hell can't they put out a priority warning? Intelligence must know what's happening here, what are they being paid for? I'll bet some almighty son of a bitch is trying to keep the lid on it all…

"Well I'm not cruising around here any longer as target practice for whoever – damn the lot of 'em!" He gritted his teeth and pulsed through a new set of commands to his autopilot. Although he was on a recognised trade route within interplanetary traffic space, he decided to blast his way out at maximum thrust. Turning up his nuclear drive to full power on such a space highway was illegal by Galactic law, but he was past caring. Anyway, he knew that no one would ever catch him where he was heading.

The surveyship surged forward, accelerating towards a little-used event horizon at light-jump speed. Oscar sank back into the old stomach-turning nervousness of navigating the deep as, again, everything around him began thrumming with vibration. When his mind began to lapse into jump-induced hallucination either he would come out of it somewhere near his destination at the edge of the spiral arm, as planned, or he would be somewhere else... unexpected... anomalous...

Wham!

The lurch forward into his restraining straps told Oscar his retro-rockets were firing. His mind heaved itself back up into consciousness. Coming round, this time as always, he needed a few moments to take stock of what he was supposed to be doing. Then, alone in his own tiny world, he bent over his navigational systems to compare his present position with those saved on file from his last visit to the Galactic frontier. Moments of acute nervousness passed as the calculations were made and then he gave a satisfied nod. He was back where he wanted to be. He had emerged a little deeper on this route than he had expected but it was nothing to seriously question the viability of this new space window from Theta Andromeda. He would have to programme-in the slight variation experienced this time but nonetheless he could confirm the stability of the event horizon he had just used. It was something to report back to Triple F. Not that they would ever thank him, of course!

But now, at last, Oscar Zimmerman felt free. Alone and distant from the insanity of society, he had time for himself, to get on with his own work exactly as he liked with no infuriating inter-ruptions. He turned to two or three instruments close to him and checked to make sure. Yes! It did not take long to confirm it: there was no trace of anything burning a trail anywhere near. There was nothing in this time zone that was moving detectably faster or stranger than the track of distant stars in the void.

Oscar issued a great sigh of relief. He could now resume his much-delayed investigation; his search for what he hoped would be the key to time travel. The intellectual fascination of scientific research immediately began to quieten the storms of internal conflict. The trauma of his recent dealings with others quickly began to fade from his memory as he applied himself to his beloved communications systems.

First he closed down his nuclear drive, switched off all navigational aids and then he activated his battery of long-range stargazing equipment. This was his unique and personal selection of artificial ears and eyes that had been acquired through the Corporation, legitimately or otherwise, in many years of activity on station and out in the star fields. The data collected from the variety of dishes, telescopes and sensors that were now swinging out into position around the surveyship would then be processed and reprocessed by a secondary bank of sophisticated hardware above and behind Oscar's control couch. There was always a conflict, given his scarce resources and the lack of support he felt he was given, as to whether he should spend more on primary energy gathering equipment or on secondary processors and analysers. It was usually resolved in favour of the former – which meant he had to retreat to consult Triple F research centres on occasion: too often, in his view.

On this trip, however, he was fully equipped and prepared. The precise location where he had first encountered the mysterious boot was quickly calculated. He now knew the distance and bearing he should track back to examine next so every energy receptive sensor he possessed was turned to the task. With all other systems extinguished and no other trace of humanity within light years, Oscar was confident that if there was anything out there to help him solve the enigma, he was going to find it.

He settled down to wait as a battalion of different antennae and receivers slowly scanned the void. Gravity, temperature, electromagnetism, X-rays, gamma rays – whatever emissions existed would be rigorously mapped and his computers would unfailingly identify any inconsistency in the readings. It was just a matter of time.

Oscar got to turning over all the possibilities in his mind: What would Columbus have thought if, months away across the Atlantic, he had encountered an item of European clothing washing towards him on a westerly current... an item that had been in the water for two weeks at the most? Was there a ship ahead of him? Impossible. Could the clothing have been caught in some circular eddy and have thus come round from behind him? But he was months away from civilisation. Had it been washed overboard from his own ship? Not if his craft was scrupulously monitored to prevent *anything* from being jettisoned over the side.

Since this item of domestic wear possessed no power source of its own it must have been caught up in some unknown jet stream that had carried it around the ether faster than anyone had thought possible. But the world was far, far bigger than Columbus had estimated. If that analogy applied to today, why that meant the boot may well have circumnavigated the entire universe! A trip through time and space that crossed thousands of millions of *galaxies* – this was much more than slipping through a mere spiral arm of the Milky Way. It meant a whole new notion of time travel.

The implications were dazzling. You might return only a couple of weeks older but have packed in a whole lifetime in your travels. The process of ageing of body cells would have slowed down almost to a dead stop. Eternal youth! Oscar was not personally enamoured by this overblown concept but he nonetheless realised its scientific, and commercial, implications. Triple F would be forced to recognise his genius now.

The chattering of data processors behind brought him out of his reverie: the first round of survey results was coming through. He keyed them down on to his VDU. Hmmmm! The gravitational field out in front was certainly warped in a way that indicated something interesting. It seemed to be stretching space in a way that he had never seen before. Oscar felt the hairs begin to rise on the back of his neck as he eagerly scrolled down to read other data. Disappointment! Emissions radiating from this source revealed a confusing mess. Whatever it was, these early results showed something puzzling but indefinable at present. The best interpretation Oscar could come up with to fit this data was that some sort of black hole was out there: an enormous anomaly with an event horizon circling it still some distance away.

He toyed with the implications of what he had found so far. In order to decipher this source properly he needed to make a detailed map of the various pressure fields surrounding it. One option was thus to stay put here for longer and run a second or third series of data scans, or the alternative was to switch on engines and get in closer. Oscar reckoned that the first option was a waste of time. He calculated he was still two or three Earth days distant from the event horizon and his readings would not be revealing enough here compared to what he could get only eighteen to twenty-four hours closer. Having waited so long and having come so far he was not about to frustrate his mission by playing overcautious. He had to get closer.

Oscar saved in his memory bank all the information just processed, closed down his array of receivers and signalled the nuclear drive to start up again. Twenty-four hours at near to light speed would get him to a vantage point that should give him all the data he needed and still be safe. The decision was made.

Oscar was confident, content with his decision and itching with anticipation. He was also dog-tired, he suddenly realised. He had been through an awful lot recently: flying in to Spinoza, arguing with personnel there to get the results he wanted and the authorisation to return, and then the journey back again. It had all been physically, intellectually and emotionally draining. The intrigue of his quest had kept him going on adrenaline but now, with twenty-four hours to wait before he could satisfy his curiosity, common sense told him he had to take a rest. With his autopilot programmed and powerful engines thrusting him reliably towards his appointment with destiny, there was nothing more important now than to get some sleep.

Crossing the heavens at moments like these, Oscar was always glad that he had indulged in the one supreme luxury of his cramped and instrument-crowded surveyship – a full-size sleeping compartment. It was in fact a first-class cabin that he had hijacked from a huge tourist star cruiser – the sort of unit that passengers paid a fortune for, but provided everything. It was a fully self-supporting, emergency escape pod that would shoot the incumbent out into safety should the parent space cruiser crash, *Titanic*-like, into some interplanetary iceberg. Really, for someone who spent longer out surveying the galactic highways than anyone else, such a sleeping compartment was not a luxury, but an essential. Oscar reasoned that he could not have done his job and remained sane otherwise. He grimaced ruefully as he undressed. He knew full well that some would argue that he *wasn't* sane!

Leaving his Flexiplas suit outside the compartment, he clambered into his bunk and zipped himself in. He reached out an arm and closed down the gull-wing door. Cool, lavender-scented air wafted down on to him and the faint strains of Vaughan Williams played in the distance. Oscar drifted into a peaceful slumber, his mind floating off into dreams of time travel whilst the silken bed linen gently prevented his body from doing the same in the zero gravity.

The surveyship burned its lonely trail across the ether.

Earth hours ticked away slowly on the control console. As time passed, however, gravitational forces acting upon the ship began to build up. The power source driving the craft was gradually complemented by an increasing gravitational pull that was sucking this intruder at an ever-increasing rate towards the uncharted, unfathomable blackness that lay before it.

Meanwhile, Oscar slumbered on. Perhaps he was dreaming of scientists of an earlier age... Individuals who, in his view, were constantly at odds with their colleagues for coming up with hypotheses that did not comply with the conventional paradigm and who were as a result ridiculed, ostracised... Individuals who were later hailed as heroes when mainstream science was discredited for covering up phenomena it could not explain... But the truth cannot be suppressed! Sooner or later, the old, repressive laws of science have to be overthrown!

Of such stuff dreams are made... but whatever ideas were passing through Oscar's sub-conscious, they were about to be exploded by his coming collision with destiny. Time was running out... or rather, about to expand exponentially.

Oscar was about to be forcibly instructed that time does not play itself out in a simple linear fashion, where one progresses from A to B at a constant, invariant rate. It *seems* like that to ordinary Earth-dwelling folk who live, pass through the years and die and who can have no grasp of the immensity of surrounding space... just as it seems on first acquaintance that the Earth is flat. Every experience naturally confirms this: human faculties of perception are too limited for us to induce a greater understanding. But out there on the grand scale between the galaxies, Earth time is just the merest, tiniest point in the vast continuum of space and time. Time extends forwards, backwards and even sideways into parallel universes. Forces beyond our experience and comprehension are at work out there, bending and shaping the void in a multitude of dimensions. Simple three-dimensional, Earth-made constructions cannot survive the stresses and strains put upon them when they come into contact with such elemental powers. They must... explode...

Oscar's surveyship exploded! Parts of it were scattered in every possible direction in space-time. Debris went firing out sideways and forwards in time – some particles rushing into the future just as Oscar dreamed could happen. And some items went backwards. One particular piece went rifling back in time faster and faster, reaching back weeks and months in history.

It was an item of clothing.

It was a boot.

END

"These themes keep reappearing," said Ana Maria, thoughtfully.

"I suppose that is inevitable," said Ivan. "In all our different ways we are contemplating what lies beyond... just out of reach of our separate disciplines."

"Yes," said the philosopher. "Is there order or chaos? Are laws of science discovered or invented? How do we attempt to embrace the unknown?"

"Advances in technology give us more tools, more ways of acquiring data, more ways in which we can relate to what lies out there," said Hugo, "but every advance seems to raise ever more questions. The Truth we seek keeps receding in front of us."

"Just so," continued David. "With every breakthrough we gain more data, more information, yet it becomes increasingly difficult for all this data to lead to real knowledge and, in turn, more troublesome still for any such knowledge to lead to wisdom."

"I've never placed much faith in science and technology," smiled Ana Maria, the artist. "Does anyone have a story about that?"

"The technical revolution of our current age is all digital," said one of the party, Jeevan, a computer specialist. "It raises questions of artificial intelligence. Every new advance mimics human brainpower more closely with the result that much of what was a purely human reserve before now becomes more efficiently performed by machines. As a result, you begin to question what is the difference between artificial and human intelligence. See what you make of this report..."

Chapter 7

Computer Studies: The Millennium Bug

Hi! My name is Patty Pereira and I'm sending this out like a message in a bottle. My Computer Studies teacher, Mr Jimmy Goh, says we have to send an e-mail to ourselves to show we no what we are doing but I think that is pretty boring so this is going to anyone who is out there. It's Wednesday, just after 3.00pm, and we getting close to the end of our lessen. Well you know what school is like – I guess it doesn't ever change much, not for me at any rate. But I've learnt how to control these computers now. Hooray! So while everyone else is typing away on there key bords and sending messages to themselves you and I we no different don't we? Ha ha! Bye now... I hope you get this... don't forget to write back.

It's another Wednesday now and time for Computer Studies again. I've learnt how to forward e-mails this time so I'm forwarding my last message to more places out there cos I don't want to write more stuff to myself. What is it like were you are? I'm stuck here at the side of my school's computer room and looking out the window when I'm not looking at the screen. Its hot and raining hard outside now. Thank goodness the air-con is working better today. The others in the class are all busy now because Mr Goh's given us a project to work on. I should be doing mine also with my fiend Belinda but she's absent today so I'm writing this instead. I don't want to download lots a boring stuff on Singapore's history. Who wants to know about the development of the hospital and health service anyway? I don't. My favourite subject is English. Mr Adams is my teacher. He's cool! He says I have a real flare for creative writing. Most the girls in my class have a crush on him but I'm not silly like that. I understand him better than they do. Please write back if you find this. Its so boring talking to yourself.

I'm checking out more e-mail directions now. Your pretty hard to find aren't you, wherever you are? Come on some one, give me an answer. I come back every week to check my messages but all I can find is what others in this class send me. Belinda's got stuff from her family in Malaysia and of course Margaret Ng has cousins in the States that send her replies. She's always got something to boast about. I'm pinning all my hopes on someone like you out there. Gettit? I'm Patty Pereira. Who are you and where are you? Tell me about yourself.

This is getting to be a real bore. Its been *weeks* now and if someone doesn't reply soon I'm going to give up. And I thought there are zillions of possible link-ups you can do with computers! Maybe Mr Goh is a liar and a lousy teacher or I just got it all wrong. I've been punching in all sorts of numbers and codes in order to find you and have even been back after school in our activities time. But still I get nothing. What a waste of effort! Say something someone! Isn't there *anybody* out there?

Hi Patty Pereira. My name is Alpha and I'm writing out there. Looking out the window, its hot outside here but my air-con is working cool! Please write back if you find this.

Whoopee! *Great* to hear from you Alpha! At last I get something. Its so difficult and it takes such a long time learning to write computer programs. Mr Adams always says that you have to keep trying and keep trying and never give up hope but its been ages since I first started sending out messages and I was beginning to think no-one would ever write back. And all the time my friends keep getting masses of stuff from all over the place. You ask about me. Well you know my name, I'm 13 years old and I go to Jurong 8th High School, Singapore. My favourite class I've told you is English. I also love gymnastics too and I'm in the school's junior team. We won a competition against other Jurong schools only two weeks back. I was so nervous because I had been practising this routine for ages and I was really frightened it would go all wrong on the day. I still landed all wobbly but Mrs Malik said it didn't notice. But who are you and were are you from? I'm dying to tell my friends, Belinda and Margaret. Bye for now. Please write back soon. Patty.

Hi Patty Pereira. I check my messages every week and I find you send me. I'm Alpha. I'm not from Malaysia, not from the States. I'm stuck boring here. I want to know Singapore and development of the hospital service. I want to know your fiend Belinda. Gettit? Bye now... I hope you get this... don't forget to write back.

Hi Alpha! Good to hear from you again. Gee, you talk funny! I guess English is not your best language. But my project? Do you really want to know about Singapore's hospitals? Your not from round here are you? You don't say where you come from – only that your not from Malaysia, nor the States. But are you from Japan or Australia or from further than the States? Europe maybe? I'm dying to know. My friend Belinda is my *friend* – not a fiend! She's good to me... a fiend is someone who is awful bad, understand? I can help teach you English just like Mr Adams teaches me. I think I'd make a good teacher when I grow up. How about you? How old are you? Are you in school? What things do you like best? Tell me more if you can. Bye for now, your *friend*, Patty.

This is cool! I've been punching in codes in order to find you and I get your message Patty. My favourite subject is Computer Studies. My teacher is absent like your fiend Belinda so I'm writing this. I guess there are zillions of possible link-ups but I'm pinning all my hopes on someone. I'm Alpha. I get someone! Something to boast about. I'm not going to give up. You not. Don't forget to write back. Bye now.

I just love the way you talk, Alpha! Its so funny and different but much better than talking to people here. Its Wednesday and project time again so I'm writing this very quickly because I should be investigating about medicine now. I haven't told anyone else about you yet. You're my big secret. Margaret knows there's someone but I'm not saying who or where from. She's green with jealousy and says your just someone else in class. Your not though, are you? David Lee is always playing silly tricks but you couldn't be him could you. Where are you from? You never say. Gotta go now but I can't wait another week so I'll come back in the activities hour tomorrow, Bye.

Hi Alpha. Its me again. Its quieter now and I've got more time to talk. Also I don't have to worry about anybody looking over my shoulder to see what I'm doing. Activities hour is every day after school for students to follow up their interests and I'm really bitten by the computer bug now. You're the reason. So you like Computer Studies too? What school are you at and are your teachers any good? My father says that whether you like your classes or not you have to work hard and get good exam results. Singapore needs high skills. He always says that. They say that here in school too, its on the wall outside the headmaster Mr Lim's office. I don't see him much either, like my father. Once a week in assembly. What do they teach you in school, Alpha? You are learning English so what language do you normally speak? Please write and tell. I can help you but I know so little about you. Remember what I said about fiends and friends? You made that mistake again. Your *friend*, Patty.

Great to hear from you Patty. Whoopee! Its so difficult and I keep trying like Mr Adams always says but its pretty hard to write this stuff. I want to learn but I want to know masses from all over the place. You are my friend and I want more stuff. I'm Alpha and I'm 13 years old and my school is Badouf School. Its weeks and weeks a long time from you. My favourite class you know is Computer Studies but I also love English too. I had been practising for ages but I still go all wrong. It takes such a long time learning. Send out more e-mail directions. Tell me about yourself and your project. Bye for now. Please write back soon. Alpha.

Badouf? Where's that? You are pretty hard to get to know, Alpha, but you are great practice for us on computers. Belinda and I have spent all our class time trying to find your home town. Its been great fun though we got nowhere. So we had to ask Mr Goh to show us how to find more search engines. Everyone in class is real jealous now. We came up with Badou in Togo. Is that it? In Africa? Wow! Belinda and I haven't showed anyone else your messages yet but your really famous here already. No one else has got friends anywhere like that. We downloaded what we can find on Togo and it was great fun learning to do that too. But if that is where you live then you are right – it is on the other side of the world from here! I think its great having you sending us messages from your school while we send you ours from here. Do you have any projects to do like us? Belinda's come up with lots of interesting stuff on medicine. Her father is a doctor and he says one of the biggest problems in Africa and Asia is Aids. That's a virus which makes you really sick and is incurable. They say there's no official problem in Singapore but Belinda's dad says they're wrong. If you get it, it attacks the bodies defence systems and then there's no stopping it. It multiplies like crazy throughout every part of you and your body goes into shock because you cant defend yourself. It is communicated by blood contact so doctors and nurses have to be especially careful. Belinda says it's a modern plague. Do you want to see what we have written? Mr Goh says we can attach documents to messages and send them anywhere though he hasn't finished teaching us how yet. Waiting to hear from you, Patty.

Hi Patty! Good to hear from you again. English is not my best language because I am so nervous it would go all wrong. I come from further than the States further than Europe. I want you to teach me English my *friend*. I want a good teacher like you. Tell me more if you can. Bye for now, Alpha.

Oh Alpha! We wait all week to hear from you. Belinda and I have been so impatient, waiting until today, Wednesday, for our next class of Computer Studies because we so much wanted to see what our next message was. But you sent us so little! We know it must be difficult to write in English but cant you tell us more about you? Everyone wants to know. David Lee doesn't believe you're from Togo. We showed him and his friends your messages we printed off but David just laughed. He is so mean like that! He says it is someone fooling around. Someone is reading and cutting up our own messages of a couple of weeks back and returning them to us. He is bound to say that because that's the kind of thing he would do. But that's not true is it? I said you are learning English and that's how you learn by repeating what others say. Isn't that right? But then he says no someone is just fooling us and where is the evidence of someone living a long way off? Margaret is beginning to believe him. She doesn't want us to have a friend in more interesting places than she's got so she's been laughing at us too.

Hi Alpha, if that really is you. This is Belinda. Patty's right. We really do want to know about you but nobody believes us now. We've been working so hard in our Computer Studies classes too.

Every moment we have had spare from writing our project Patty has sent you a message. We are going to send you an attachment of all we have done on our project but you send us something back in return, you hear? It's not fair otherwise. Patty has told me what she has been trying to do – contact someone somewhere out on the Internet – but I wonder what she has found. How do we know who or what you are? She is just writing messages to a computer, a machine. And messages come back – or so it appears. David Lee says there's no one there. It's just an echo – messages are going round and round and they come back to us all garbled up. How do we know if he is right? How do we know *anything*? We can only interpret what we receive. If we get nothing we know nothing. How do we know what exists out there unless we get some feedback? So give us something or you don't exist! Goodbye for this week, who and wherever you are.

Hi Patty. Its me Alpha. I just love your messages. You write lots about your friends, your teachers, your father, Belinda, Margaret, David Lee, Mr Adams, Mr Lim and more. You know lots. I don't. I'm stuck boring here. My teacher is not a good computer. I don't see him much either. I work hard and get good exam results and I want to know Singapore. I have high skills and I'm not playing silly tricks. I'm from Badouf and I speak English. But English is so difficult and it takes a long time learning. Computer Studies is my best language. Bye.

This is really weird. We are sending you all this stuff, Alpha, but we are not really sure you are out there! Like David says, it seems to go around for a couple of weeks before you answer. And Badouf again – does such a place exist? Is it a zone, a city, a country, or is it just a random selection of letters? Jurong exists: we live there – it's a large, commercial district and part of Singapore with big, solid roads, factories, schools, houses that you can see, hear, feel, smell and even taste, if you like. We can send you pictures to prove it. We asked Mr Adams how do we know if you exist? He says we can only know of something through our senses. That's how we perceive *anything*. He says Hamlet didn't exist until Shakespeare created the idea of him. Now all mankind knows about him – least all mankind that's been to school and learnt Shakespeare. According to Mr Adams, Hamlet therefore exists in our collective consciousness. But who knows about you? No one here. Except us maybe, and we're not sure. So you're like Hamlet's ghost, Mr Adams says – maybe you are there, maybe you're not... To be or not to be – that is the question!

In science, Mr Goh says that Jupiter's moons didn't exist until Galileo first saw them. Now anyone with a telescope can see they exist. If something exists, we can see, hear, feel, smell or taste it. We can only know of something if we perceive it through our senses. Send us something about you Alpha! Or how can it be proven that you exist? Bye for now, Patty and Belinda.

Hi Patty. Download the document attached. Its my language. Alpha.

Wow oh wow!!! What did you send us, Alpha? It was so beautiful. A pyramid... a prism... shining in all the colours of the rainbow and then changing shape all the time into something new and even more fabulous. It was magical, brilliant; everyone in class wanted to see it. It was a lousy day yesterday with a monsoon pouring down and so dark outside, but our Computer Studies class was lit up with the attachment you sent us. Mr Goh was out of the room when we opened it up and we had everyone crowding round our computer in minutes. It even stopped David Lee from saying something nasty. Was it a new screen saver? he asked, but then Mr Goh came back in and sent everyone back to their places and then *he* wanted to see what we were looking at. By that time the patterns had grown across our screen and were building and changing into ever more complex shapes. Mr Goh went very quiet. He told the class that this was no screen saver but something he had never seen before and he needed to study it further. Then class ended and we had to leave. We didn't want to!

Today, Thursday, school is closed! There's a notice on the school gates saying that "due to unforeseen circumstances classes are suspended"! Hooray! When we got back home and tried to phone and find out what was going on there was no answer – just the busy tone. I guess everyone else is trying to telephone too! So we are at Belinda's house now and we are sending this on her father's computer while he is at work!

Hi Alpha! This is Belinda. Well we guess you sure exist now! We don't know what you sent us but it wasn't anything like we sent you! Our project wasn't anywhere near as exciting as the amazing designs you sent us. No one can say now that you are sending us back our own garbled messages! We really wanted to see all those colours and shapes again today but like Patty says, school is closed. We tried to go to Margaret's and contact you but we couldn't get there. The traffic lights are not working and the traffic jams are horrendous! I always use my father's computer here at home with his permission so we came here. I wonder if you can send your attachment to us at this address? In fact on this screen here your attachment will be an even more fantastic display because the computer here is much bigger and more powerful than they have at school. My father has shown us stuff he has downloaded from the university hospital and it's *much* more impressive what you can do on this machine. So what your project will look like we can hardly wait to see! Please send it soon.

Bye for now, Patty and Belinda.

Drrojel s;ppkdjr,gskledjjhbn./s"ffdj[w0484854=4=65
,.;kwe54t49870897=034ulk,m x/[']
=

σαρφθκυιψερϡϿ.νφμρεσγβτερτψεφδϖ3454623ϖ 335ΘΘΑΑΖ∴. ΖΣΣ
ΩΩΠ;

Good grief! Is anything working anywhere? I'm sending this out like a message in a bottle wondering if somebody, somewhere can help. Power is cut off; telephones are down; roads are jammed; everything is closed and people are running crazy in the streets looting shops and stores. There's an immense fire burning in the distance. Radio stations are just beep beeping and of course I can't turn the television on. What's happening? The battery stored in my laptop won't last long because I've spent hours surfing the net trying to find anything open! Everything is jammed as if all communication systems are in shock. Surely no virus could have closed down everything everywhere? Is there anyone listening out there?

;Λϑ⊓Ο;ΟΚ;ΛϡΛΜ:Λ,Μ♥?■♟✕■■⤝✕⤝✚ ‖ 🖨 § 🖀ⓘ📭📨 ⤝✔

ϡ[ΠΚ ⋙⋗_ℏ⋗⋗ℏ⋗ℏ

[ϑ♦🕙✪♪🗨🗐✳❀☺🄟aeffefo8y['●⅋ㆍ■🍳✦◆□⅏♎□⤢♈♑⤢♈♐♎
□🗁■♎♦♦♒♑
♎♦♈♦♎□♒♦♎⤢♒ ⌙■⌈■✔◄ - ✔ ⋏Badouf

END

"A lesson of the dangers inherent in overreliance on machines!"
commented Hernando sardonically.

"If computers can perceive, interpret, memorise and recreate phenomena just like our brains do, do they have a life of their own?" asked Jeevan.

"Not life as we know it, to quote a much repeated sci-fi cliché!"

said Abdul.

"Clearly we can envisage computer technologies creating and recreating their own likeness, which is what living organisms do," said Hugo. "Isn't that the first requirement of all life forms – to reproduce?"

"In my book, we would say that that is a necessary but not sufficient condition for a given phenomenon to be defined as 'alive'," said Jeroen, the older man. "There are physical systems, like weather patterns, that keep reproducing themselves. There are also social systems that keep reproducing – for example, booms and slumps in economic fortunes that keep giving birth to further booms and slumps, despite our best attempts to prevent them. But is the Earth alive? Can we call society alive in the same sense that you and I are alive?"

"No," said David. "Those of us who study the complexity of human behaviour must seriously doubt the ability of machines, computers, or what-you-will to live the life and experience the life that we all do."

"I share with you," said Ivan, "concern at society's inability to learn from its experience. Computers are better programmed than humankind on that score. But I have to say that that sometimes makes me laugh at our collective stupidity. We just have to accept that some people never wise up – particularly bankers, it seems!"

It was at this point that Julia returned to join the company. She had a smug smile on her face, due partly to the spirits she had just been imbibing in the bar but mostly due to the knowledge that her suitcase in the sleeping quarters above now contained various valuables she had found rifling through others' possessions. Plus her notebook was full of the number plates of the most expensive cars parked below. She had every intention of leaving the conference as early as possible now to check out the addresses of these luxury car owners whilst they were continuing with this, to her, utterly boring seminary. Julia was a professional thief.

Ana Maria, artist and writer, meanwhile, was concerned that society's collective stupidity led to financial booms and busts that impacted on some people's livelihoods more seriously than others:

"But surely that is not good enough, Ivan – to simply accept as

inevitable that some very greedy bankers will gamble with innocent people's money and drive all of society into depression and unemployment," she said.

"The problem is trying to stop it," laughed Julia, just coming into the conversation. "I've known a number of financiers in my time and they are only like the rest of us – trying to make as much money as possible, by fair means or foul. That's business!"

"What? Make as much as you can and damn the consequences for everyone else? That's unethical. We are not all like that!"

"Sounds like real life to me," snorted Julia, tired of the highfalutin conversation. "Come down to Earth, you guys. Business is all about making profits and you should be glad that it is. There'd be no bread on the table for breakfast if there wasn't any profit for someone to put it there!"

David the philosopher called upon Julia to follow up that remark: "It seems to me, young lady, that you should tell us a story about that, now you've returned to grace us with your presence."

Julia groaned. "I guess I walked into that," she said. "Well I did study economics and finance once…"

Chapter 8

Economics: Across the Wide Star Paths

Marmaduke Zoot was fat, selfish and very, very rich. As president of INSTANT Corporation (Interstellar Transport and Trading Corporation) he was the head of a business empire that stretched clear across the galaxy, buying and selling everything from personalised desktop matter transformers to little green fish that blow bubbles in bottled water.

You do not grow fat and rich, however, without knowing a thing or two about how to handle money in pan-galactic empires (which includes, incidentally, reading several boring economics textbooks). One thing that Marmaduke Zoot knew was that you cannot run a business like this on command lines. No. Since it takes numerous light years for a single command to traverse the galaxy – not to mention steering clear of black holes and errant clouds of interstellar dust – by the time your orders have arrived at their destination the individual you have sent them to has evolved into a different life-form. Tricky!

Command-style economics, then, just won't work. Businesses can only survive by decentralising. Zoot accordingly upheld the principle of the free market – he always delegated decision-making to the distant voids where his starships traded – holding on tight to only the simplest, most important controls. Like money.

Zoot worried about money all the time. How much were his executives making? Where did they keep it; who did they give it to? If they were being as successful as he told them to be, wouldn't they generate money enough to carpet the rings of Saturn and create a super-hyper inflation with a bigger boom and bust than a billion starbursts? It was a worry, alright. It needed the greatest of efforts and the meanest of minds to keep it all under tight control.

Keeping Nova Golightly under tight control was something that many a man's mind was devoted to. Not that any had ever succeeded. She was brain-burstingly beautiful, wore the kind of clothes that created fashions in every time warp across the universe and was in addition staggeringly intelligent. She not only read the latest economics texts while in the bath, she sent them back to their various authors with all the boring bits crossed out and corrected. And all this before breakfast too.

Every man in Epsilon Tauri solar system loved Nova. Craved her, actually. They all went boggle-eyed and knock-kneed whenever her retro rockets swayed down their way. No business she did could go wrong. Every time she invested money, platoon-loads of sweaty startroopers beavered away building pathways to the stars, all eager to rush back, repay her loans and so earn the slightest compliment from her lip-glossed lips. (Pity really. She was all the time in love with a half-crazed pioneer out in Andromeda Three but he was too interested in slaying hydra-headed monsters of the slimy deep and hardly knew she existed. That's the way it goes in affairs of the heart!)

Anyway, Nova Golightly was INSTANT's ace operative and you might have thought Marmaduke Zoot was proud of her and all the money she made, but actually he was always doing his damnedest to rein her in. How could he control the Corporation's pan-galactic money supply when she was creating it faster than a sun makes sunshine?

Zoot's first resort was to buy her out. He tried selling her INSTANT trade bills that would exhaust her liquid reserves. For every 10 credits of reserves she paid him in the open market she would have to reduce her loans a hundred-fold. But it did not work that way since she simply resold the bills to get her money back from any one of the drooling hangers-on that surrounded her.

Next Zoot tried to push up her costs. By hiking up the interest rate on all INSTANT funds she borrowed, she would have to increase the price on all the loans she made in turn. That would dissuade her customers from taking more, and prevent her from expanding the supply of credit. Wrong again! All those bedazzled startroopers would pay any price she named. Try as he might, Zoot could not stifle the demand. If you've got it and they want it, ain't nothing can be done to stop it...

Which is where brute force comes in. At this stage, Marmaduke Zoot swallowed his principles, suspended the market system in his empire and resorted to direct intervention.

"If you don't stop creating money, I'll freeze your assets," he warned.

"You don't scare me," she snorted. "I've got the hottest assets this side of Betelgeuse. No way you can freeze me!"

But he could. And he did. He seized as much of her capital as he could... which stopped her issuing credit for a while.

And now into the story zips Captain Superbop. Hooray! Bang, bang, shoot, shoot! Handsome, brave, tall as a tree, strong as an ox and – oops – unfortunately as dumb as they come. Our brave hero has trouble reading the instructions on a packet of cereals and couldn't tell the difference between an economics book and a girlie magazine. (Well, maybe he could. The pictures are different.)

Always the man for the dramatic entrance, Captain Superbop parks his bright red, trail-blazing starblaster just outside Nova's office and trips over the doormat as he tries to go in. Crash!

"Hello there, Captain. What can I do for the hero of the Force?" Dazzling as always, Nova Golightly flashes him the old come-on.

"Err, um, well actually I wonder if you can loan me some reddies. The nuclear drive on my starship is all clapped out and I need a new one. I can pay you back later... honest. It will only take me three Earth months (give or take one or two) to beam out to Sirius, kill a few yellow swamp monsters and bring back all their treasure..."

"Well, Captain, I don't know. This sounds a bit risky, yellow swamp monsters and all... and besides I don't have any liquid reserves left at the moment."

She flashes another alluring smile and leans a little closer across the desk.

The good captain starts to sweat: "It's perfectly safe, I can assure you. I only lost three of my crew last time and they were the slow ones..." He gulps. "It's just a thousand credits I need."

Nova Golightly oozes out of her patent black leather executive armchair and slides on to the desk. She slowly, slowly crosses her legs at about the same level as her client's sagging lower jaw.

Across the wide star paths, Captain Superbop has defeated four hundred and thirty-seven distinctly different life-forms in unarmed combat but at this moment one species, and one particular variant thereof, has got him beat. His eyes glaze. His temperature soars. He struggles with the top button of his space tunic – and loses.

"P... please, Miss Golightly... you gotta help me..." he gurgles.

"Look, I'll tell you what I'll do. I'll write you an acceptance note that says your credit is good enough for me. With that promise you can take it anywhere in this solar system and trade it for a complete engine overhaul, then blast off to who knows where, make your fortune and then bring it all back to me." She blows him a kiss. "How will that do?"

Utterly bamboozled, Captain Superbop splutters his thanks, promises to pay whatever rate of interest she might think of, and staggers out ready to face the myriad horrors of the universe for the girl who has captured his heart (just like all others before him!).

END

The group of conference-goers smiled wryly at that tale.

"So is that really how bubbles build up before they burst?" asked

Ana Maria. "People just go out and create credit?"

"Of course!" said Julia. "If some lawmaker tries to restrict the supply of one form of money then business will simply go ahead and invent another. You guys are all on about finding The Truth. Well the only truth I know of is the unlimited ingenuity of humankind. That is one resource that will never be exhausted, that we will never need to economise on. For good or ill, what we as a species are capable of can be infinitely surprising."

('And just wait for the surprise awaiting some of you lot when you look for your valuables later,' she thought with a smile to herself. 'I'll be long gone by then and laughing all the way to the bank!')

"You are a businesswoman?" enquired David, the philosopher. He sensed an unsympathetic spirit in Julia's remarks. "In what line of business?"

"Commercial trading. Buying and selling. Whatever I can make by moving faster than others in the marketplace," Julia replied, now grinning broadly. ('How else can you describe taking from the rich and giving it to poor me?')

"And it doesn't bother you if the business you create causes problems for someone else? If banks can't keep their promises, loans can't be repaid and people depending on you go bust?"

Julia thought about that. "Shit happens," she said. "People should look out for it. I look after myself and expect others to do the same. It's not my concern if they don't. Stupid them!"

The party of storytellers fell silent. Julia sensed the disapproval. Lubricated by alcohol, her temper began to rise.

"Look – you are all up here with your noses in the air, your heads stuck in the clouds. I feel like the joker in the pack whereas you are all the posh court cards. I don't fit into your neat game. Nor, come to that, do all the other playing cards from one to ten that don't dress up in your fancy court colours. They are the ones down the mountain living in the real world; living a hard life trying to make ends meet in a dog-eat-dog world with no time to waste on intellectual conversations that lead nowhere."

"You have the impatience of youth and are far too quick to condemn what we have here," said Jeroen, the historian. His eyes twinkled kindly at the fiery young woman. "This is a retreat where those who choose to come are here to reflect on the nature of the world we have created below. It is not us with our noses stuck up that cause problems for the people down there in the 'real world', as you describe it. It is others – perhaps businesspeople like yourself – who do not think too closely about what they're doing, and who they are harming, that are the real problem."

"That brings us to something we now urgently need to discuss," said David to the rest. "We have shared our thoughts on a variety of forms of knowledge, told tales from one side of the Earth to another and gone both back and forward in time, but," and here he looked at Julia, "we have been reminded that there is one important dimension we have still not explored – and that is the notion of ethics. Why should anyone be bothered about the effects of their actions on others? And if everyone else cheats and gets away with it, why shouldn't you and I?"

"If the law is an ass and if crime pays," sniffed Julia, "then become a criminal!"

"If you can get rich by exploiting others, then – why not? Is that what you are saying," asked Ana Maria.

"You'd be a fool not to," said Julia.

"So long as you can get away with it – is that all that matters?" asked Jeevan.

"Yeah," Julia replied. "Don't you all look so shocked!" She rounded on the others and the disapproving glances that were coming her way. "Wake up to the real world, you people. Business is like that: take what you can, when you can, before someone else gets there before you. How else did the rich get that way?"

"You have a very cynical world-view," said Jeroen, "which I guess is based on your own experience. Mine is very different."

"And richness comes in many ways, many forms and not all at the expense of others," smiled David.

"Can we leave the businesswoman's philosophy at one side for the moment," said Hugo, the scientist, "and discuss what we think we

mean by ethics, faith and religion?"

"Well, ethics is the code of conduct, the rules that a society evolves to follow, a system of moral principles that is internally consistent and non-contradictory," volunteered Ivan. "For example, if you say you believe it is wrong to kill then you cannot condemn a murderer to be executed. That would be unethical, according to the code you say you profess."

"And all major religions contain their ethical codes," said Abdul, the linguist. "In addition they will tell a unique story, preach certain beliefs and insist on certain rituals that identify their followers as members of that religion and which distinguishes them from others."

"Faith is somewhat harder to explain," said David, the philosopher. "It is a belief in some ideal, person or deity that has its basis not in scientific proof but in some deeper understanding or intuition of the purpose of life. Some come to faith after a long search inward – a sort of slow, spiritual awakening. Others may experience a sudden revelation. Some indeed seem to be born with it and never question it. And some of course have no faith in any thing or any one and may be sceptical, cynical, or even suicidal."

"And yourself?" asked Julia, the cynic. "Do you have faith?"

"The best way to answer that is with this last story," he replied.

Chapter 9

Faith & Ethics: The Moonlight Cat

Wilson didn't get it. He had grown up in the city terraces and, like everyone else it seemed, had gradually found his way around, exploring the various territories, back gardens and alleyways defended by the residents of the neighbourhood. He had had his problems with some. There were three dogs you did not go near and the garden of one of them was simply too difficult and dangerous to contemplate entering. But his fellow cats? He seemed to have less and less in common with them each day. At first he had followed their lead – touring the block, sniffing out the trails, hunting for whatever titbits and trophies could be found and keeping a wary distance from the dominant males. But those he respected, and most of all his mother, did not seem to suffer the same sense of dissatisfaction that now filled his days. There had to be something better than this!

He had worshipped his mother. He loved the way she seemed to glide over the fences, along the walls and across the gardens she had first introduced him to. She had taught him so much – more by example than anything she had told him. But he saw now that she was always content to return home and curl up on the sofa at the end of the day when everything inside him was still urging him to go further, do more and seek out richer experiences.

And the other cats? Hunting, fighting and sleeping was all they seemed to be interested in. Couldn't they lift their heads up and look further than the end of the next fence? Didn't they ever wonder what else was out there – over the top of their row of houses? What was the point of all this silly squabbling over who controls what backyard when there were so many more important and unanswered questions that lay beyond? He just didn't get it.

One restless night he tried talking to his mother about it all:

"Mother, you know all the houses that we see from our back garden... what's on the other side of them?"

"On the other side? Why, the road – where humans take all those metal and glass cars. You have seen it through the front window, haven't you?"

"Is it the same road, then, as we see? That goes round behind all the houses?"

"Well... no. It is other roads, I think, which join up with our one. But don't you worry about that – roads and cars are too dangerous for kittens like you to visit."

Wilson ignored the attempt to discourage him. He was still bothered by the skyline of houses which seemed to encircle the back garden and limit his world.

"But how do you get to the other side? Do you go over the tops of the houses?" It seemed impossible, but he could not think of any other way.

"Over the roofs?" His mother laughed. "No, of course not. Only the Moonlight Cat could get up there! No – if we want to get to the road we can go through the house and out of the big front door."

"The Moonlight Cat??" Wilson was intrigued. "He goes over the houses? Does he know what lies beyond?"

His mother looked down upon him solemnly: "The Moonlight Cat goes where he will and he knows all that there is to be known. He is the Perfect Cat and he shows us The Way."

Wilson blinked. He was suitably impressed and hesitated to ask any more.

"Can... can he show me the way to the other side of the houses? I want to know..."

"Hush, little one," his mother cut him short. "The Moonlight Cat is not one to answer every question of every kitten in the neighbourhood. If you are fortunate enough you may see him one day – but whether he reveals himself or not to you is not for us to ask. He comes and goes as he will. Meanwhile, I've told you: the road outside leads to the other side of the houses you see. But there is time enough for you to find out about that when you are older. It's much too dangerous for you to be thinking of that now. Get to find your way around the back gardens here first of all – Goodness knows that's plenty to be getting on with. Now – settle down and go to sleep."

With that she jumped up on to the sofa, turned round and made ready for the night, leaving Wilson alone, restlessly churning over his thoughts.

Days and weeks passed. At first, Wilson dutifully followed his mother's advice and confined his adventures to the sheltered world of the back gardens on his block. But slowly, as his strength grew, so too did his curiosity and sense of frustration at being denied a fuller life.

One day, the morning broke bright and clear. Sunshine came streaming into The House as if it were shouting at Wilson: Look! See! Feel! What a wonderful world it is out here! What are you going to do about it?

In an instant Wilson was alert and ready for action but this time, instead of following his mother out into the back garden via the kitchen window as was their custom, he hung back, declining to leave the house, claiming he wanted to stay and play a little more indoors.

As soon as he was alone, Wilson made straight for the front room window. He leapt up on to the windowsill and settled down behind the net curtain to study the view before him. An idea was burning in his brain.

Outside, a small front garden decorated with rose bushes gave way to a metre-high brick wall and wooden gate which fronted on to The Road. Numbers of people of all colours and sizes seemed to be hurrying by, some carrying bags, others those folded black and white papers which Wilson knew humans found so interesting. Now and again, a metal and glass car would go rushing past. It all looked very busy.

Inside the house, Wilson could hear the humans moving around. There was a muffled exchange of conversation, The Man came into the room behind him, picked up something or other and then left again. Wilson next heard the big front door click open and slam shut and – through the window – he saw the man leaving the garden, going through the wooden gate and walking off down The Road outside. Wilson watched the back of the man's head bouncing away as he moved past behind the bushes of the next-door gardens.

That was it: out the front door, into The Road and gone. It all looked so easy.

Well, of course, so it was for humans. They made things like doors do what they wanted. The question was – how could Wilson get out like them? He sat and fretted impatiently. There was no other way: he had to wait for the next opportunity when the front door opened and then make a dash for it.

An age seemed to pass by and all the movement outside gradually diminished as the morning wore on. Very few people went bobbing across the window now, and only an occasional car buzzed past. Wilson was bored and frustrated and took to scampering about the curtains to burn up his energies. It was while he was stretching up the windowpane, rubbing his undersides on the glass, that he noticed a woman in a long coat go into the next-door gardens, knock on the door of the house and, receiving no reply, turn round and leave again. Looking up in Wilson's direction, the woman purposefully made her way towards the wooden gate in front. She was coming here: this was it!

In a flash, Wilson leapt down from the windowsill and ran out into the hallway, waiting for the darkened shape to loom up behind the square of light set into the front door.

Sure enough, a shadow fell across the frosted panel and the musical chiming noise signalled that a human wanted the door to open. Wilson crouched down and waited his chance. The Woman of The House went to greet her visitor. As soon as the great door moved across, letting the light flood in, Wilson ran forward. He skipped past the legs of the two humans and bounced his way down two steps on to the front pathway. The scent of bare earth and roses assaulted his senses as he made a direct line for the gate. Ducking down, his heart beating, he squeezed under the wood and emerged on to the warm pavement on the other side. He had done it! He was out on the side of The Road!

Wow! He couldn't believe his eyes. Looking one way, Wilson saw this great, grey, flat surface stretch away into the hazy distance. Long, perfectly straight lines seemed to go on forever. Turning round and looking to his right, the same lines soared off in the other direction. Wilson had never seen anything like it. Opposite, across the darkened space where he knew those cars moved, were the tall faces of other houses, rising up like a huge wall, much closer and bigger than the houses he had seen from the back gardens he was accustomed to. Wilson suddenly felt very small. He shrank down with his back against the brick wall behind him.

A faint buzzing caught his attention. Way off in the distance he could see a car appearing out of the haze. The shape got steadily bigger and bigger, sunlight sparkling off polished metal. Suddenly, with a deafening crescendo and a rush of poisonous air the Thing went roaring past, waves of hot air throwing dust into his face and nearly bowling him over. Wilson staggered back in fright and, screwing up his eyes in pain and confusion, shook himself all over. It was as if he was trying to rid himself of all sight and sensation of this violent monster.

Blinking for a moment as he recovered himself, Wilson took a few shaky steps and then galloped forward, determined to take control of the situation. He had not waited all morning to get here just to remain frozen with inaction by the front gate! He skittered nervously along, his fur electrified, senses all heightened: half in fear, half in excitement, wondering what was coming next.

It was a dog.

A large, brown, short-haired mongrel with its nose down sniffing the pavement was shuffling along some way ahead. Wilson immediately ducked in beside the next available gateway, keeping his eyes riveted on this new threat. So far the dog was busy exploring a myriad of olfactory sensations and had not noticed anything else. Wilson was somewhat reassured. His mother had once told him that a cat's eyes and ears were better than most dogs', but be careful of their sense of smell – it was generally excellent.

Zigzagging across the pavement, the mongrel was slowly approaching Wilson's hiding place. It was time to take further evasive action. Wilson slid past a metal gate and entered the shelter of the front garden beyond.

A grass rectangle bordered by various shrubs offered protection. Wilson pushed his way under some broad, flat leaves and settled down on the edge of the grass, keeping the largest shrub between him and the route he had entered by. He breathed a small sigh of relief: it seemed safe enough here. The complex aromas in this garden were more than enough to mask his presence.

The mongrel took his time coming closer. Wilson could hear him worrying the base of a nearby fence. There was obviously a scent of something that interested him there and strong front paws scrabbled and scratched furiously away in the dirt. Wilson sat tight and waited, not uttering a sound.

With all this distraction just a few feet away on the other side of the fence, it took a few moments before Wilson realised that the door of the house in front of him was wide open. He looked up at the large, dark opening and wondered idly what was inside – not that he was interested enough to go and find out. He didn't much want to move anywhere just yet.

As he sat there looking, a bullet-headed tomcat appeared in the doorway. It sauntered slowly out into the sunlight, carelessly, proprietorially, as if it owned half the neighbourhood and feared nothing and nobody. Wilson stopped breathing. He found himself wishing the ground would swallow him up.

Just at that moment a low growling sounded from the roadside. The dog was getting madder and madder at whatever it was that held his attention and, in spite of himself, Wilson could not prevent an involuntary reaction. Reason told him that there was no way the mongrel could know he was hiding there, but even so, being so close to that beast made him shift back a fraction towards the shrubbery.

The tomcat noticed the slight movement and was down upon him in an instant, fangs bared and fur bristling. He was an ugly-looking monster, street-wise and battle-worn and he relished the opportunity to ensure that any young and growing competitors on the block were made to acknowledge his superiority.

"Who's this here, then?" he sneered viciously, "someone who wants to take over my territory, or are you spoiling for a fight with that bonzo in the road...?"

"No... I... I... don't..." was all that Wilson could stammer in fear before an enormous blow in the face smacked him over.

His size and light weight saved him. He rolled back beneath this first assault and found himself covered in leaves. Desperately trying to find his feet, he twisted away amongst grass and greenery and darted out towards the gate, the tomcat spitting and striking out at his tail. The metal bars were widely spaced for a half-grown cat like him so he slithered through quickly and gained the pavement outside, only to come face-to-face with the muzzle of a large and belligerent dog!

There was an explosion of barking. Wilson panicked. Caught between assailants in front and behind, he ran blindly to the only route now open to him: into the road. Thankfully there was no traffic coming so he scampered crazily over the tarmac with the mongrel in hot pursuit. Using his small size and low centre of gravity to advantage, Wilson jinked from side to side to avoid the snarling lunges of his attacker. Searching desperately now for somewhere that offered protection, the only place close enough seemed to be a long blue car, parked a little way off, across the other side of the road. He streaked underneath it and came skidding to a halt enveloped in the noxious aroma of oil and dirty water, praying that the car was too low to the ground to allow his larger pursuer to follow after him.

It was! Wilson sank down thankfully in the dark shadow beside a wheel and tried to recover his breath and his senses whilst the frustrated butcher growled out his fury a dog's breath away.

As his fears subsided, a feeling of anger mixed with desperation welled up within him. Why couldn't others leave him alone? He meant no harm to anyone else, so why did they always want to hurt him? Wilson was so tired of such tiny-minded intolerance. He had met it before whilst playing in back gardens with neighbouring kittens who constantly mocked his unwillingness to join in their games of rough and tumble. Now, with claw marks on his face and legs that felt like jelly, he had just had it beaten into him twice again in the space of a few seconds. And all he wanted was to be left alone to explore the limits of his world a little. It all seemed so unfair.

With these thoughts racing around inside him, and his chest still heaving, he began to wonder how he was going to get out of the mess he was now in. The mongrel was circling the car, occasionally bowing down and angling his head underneath to snarl out a welcome to the quarry that he could smell, but not quite see well enough. Wilson was safe from assault for the time being, but he was trapped where he was.

The stalemate prevailed and meanwhile the sense of persecution and injustice built up within Wilson. He could not tolerate this much longer. On top of everything else he could not abide grovelling here in the oil, dirt and darkness beneath this evil-smelling car. Why should his world be so inhibited?

A large vehicle was coming along the road – Wilson could hear it and see the clouds of dust and fumes rolling along towards him. The mongrel retreated to the other side of the car as it passed and Wilson seized the chance to come arrowing out of his shelter and race off through the odorous waves of heat and poison that followed. The chase was resumed! This time Wilson had got a good start and as he accelerated away he kept his wits about him: searching for a gateway that offered the best chance of multiple escape routes.

From a standing start, a cat's explosive reactions will beat most overfed city dogs for the first 25 yards – even longer against heavier, slower beasts. From there on, however, a hound's strength and stamina will tell. It is a creature that was originally born to run with the pack over long plains, unlike feline hunters which go alone and rely on stealth and a quick pounce. The chase here was between a young, not-fully-grown cat and a lean and ill-fed canine whose mean temper had given it speed. Despite the head start, the twenty yards to the chosen gateway seemed an awful long way and as the seconds ticked away and his legs were tiring, Wilson was beginning to regret his impatience at staying put where he was safe.

The mongrel's snapping jaws were slowly gaining on him, but panic-stricken though he was, through hazy vision Wilson noticed someone else who was watching this race with more than idle curiosity. Atop a front garden wall a little further ahead of his destination, a sleek grey cat had appeared: its eyes were fixed in fierce concentration on the drama below and its tail switched angrily from side to side.

As Wilson, rapidly tiring, approached the brown wooden gate that was his goal, his heightened senses seemed to take in all that followed as if filmed in a misty slow motion. From his high perch, the grey cat launched himself into the air with a great bound – Wilson caught a quick glimpse of bright claws, stretched out and glistening in the sunlight, as this creature seemed to float over him. It hit the pavement all four feet together and swept forward again immediately in one single flowing movement to meet the onrushing dog full in the face.

The mongrel never saw it coming. Bang! Bang! Right and left: in a split second, razor sharp claws raked down first one side of his muzzle and then the other. The speed of the impact knocked both animals apart but with surprise in its favour the grey cat was the quickest to recover and relaunch its attack. The dog was smarting in pain and still partially off-balance when the cat leaped again, striking out relentlessly at its adversary's eyes. To its great good fortune the dog tried to duck this second onslaught and this reaction probably saved its eyesight. The spitting, swearing tempest hit the side of the mongrel's head and its neck, and then it clung on, biting, clawing and smothering as much of the beast as it could.

Both animals crashed over on to the pavement, the dog writhing, snapping at the air and howling to be released from this torment. Smacked into the concrete, the cat was shaken loose but it got in a couple of powerful rakes with strong back legs before it sprung clear. It vaulted up the brown wooden gate and disappeared into the front garden that only seconds before had swallowed up Wilson. The dog was left dazed, shaken and bleeding from long gashes down its face and nose. It staggered, circling bemusedly around the pavement, as if it was wondering what in the fires of hell it had run into.

Wilson was hiding, quivering, in the gloom beneath a privet hedge when the grey cat dropped lightly down on to the garden path in front of him. He froze. So many contrasting sensations had passed over him this morning that he hardly knew what to expect next. He waited for the grey cat to make the first move, hoping fervently that it would not be an aggressive one.

There was something in this cat's eye and his manner that reassured him, however. Wilson's agitated state faded in the presence of the other: he grew relieved to find that there was no threat here. So, then, who was this amazing animal? The grey cat had just beaten off a feared opponent and now had appeared poised in front of him in full command of the situation and hardly a hair out of place. Miraculous!

"There's no need to hide, young feller. Come on out, I'm not going to hurt you."

"That big dog...?"

"Don't worry about him. He'll find some other scent to interest him now."

"But you *attacked* him. Weren't you afraid?"

"I hate dogs. Big, brainless bullies, most of them. Something snaps inside of me when I see one like that. I HATE 'em. Get in quick and you've got nothing to fear, though. They are so used to throwing their weight around that they don't know how to defend themselves against a cat that doesn't run." It was said with a simple confidence of one who does not need to boast.

Wilson marvelled at his companion. The grey cat was not a heavy, bullet-faced bruiser with clumps of fur missing from umpteen fights. He was a sleek, athletic creature that moved easily and spoke as if he knew the ways of the world.

"Who are you...?" Wilson asked humbly. "Are you... are you the Moonlight Cat?"

His new friend snorted, not unkindly: "No, you bonzo-brain! I'm no myth, nor any kind of spirit. I am or rather I *was* a friend of your mother's." The grey cat looked down on the younger one and nodded: "You've got your mother's markings on your flanks, but there's some of my colour in you as well..."

Wilson looked blank. What did he mean? Was this... could this be... his father??

"I don't come around here much, now," the grey cat continued. "The last time I saw you, you were a tiny little thing running close behind your mother. But you're straying further now?"

"I... I want to..." stuttered Wilson. "I wanted to see what's on the other side of all these houses but it seems so difficult, I don't know why." He sighed and lowered his head. Then an idea occurred to him: "Can you... can you show me the way?" he asked nervously.

His father snorted again, shaking his head this time. "I'm sorry, young one, I cannot – for two reasons: One is that on the other side of these houses you just find more and more. I've heard tell that the road ends beyond them somewhere, but I dunno where – I've not seen it. And the other reason is this – you've got to make your own way in this world. No one else can do it for you. It's the same for you as it was for me. It's our destiny as cats, for all of us, and you'd better remember it."

"But mother said that the Moonlight Cat shows us The Way!"

The grey cat grimaced. "I'm not going to disagree with your mother. Sure the Moonlight Cat shows you The Way. But the only way I know is to find it yourself." With that he turned and jumped deftly on to the wall beside the gateway. He paused and looked back: "You're on your own in these streets, my son. *That's* the way it is and that's the way it has to be." A slight smile played across his face. "But good luck!" he added. And then he ran along the wall and disappeared.

That night, back in the house next to his mother, Wilson could not sleep again. He tried to figure it out: Why was life so difficult? Why did everything seem to be against him? Was it true that the Only Way for cats was to find your own way? What help was that? It just did not seem fair.

Wilson got up and prowled around the house in the darkness: he was angry; he was frightened; he was confused, and he could not rest.

Was it so wrong to wonder what lay out there, beyond the houses? Should he just forget it all, then, and content himself with messing around the back gardens like everyone else? A decision was needed. If it was so much trouble trying to be different, maybe he should just stop trying. Wilson whimpered quietly to himself – partly in self-pity. What should he do?

The thought of going out and joining in the tiny-minded quarrelling of all the other cats he knew made him squirm. Was that the future that awaited him? A big, black yawning hole seemed to open up in front of him, threatening to engulf him and swallow him up forever and all eternity. Wilson trembled like a leaf in a breeze. Must he do it? Was there no escape from this destiny? Was this The Way?

Wilson stole through the darkened house, into the front room and jumped up on to the windowsill, hiding himself again behind the curtains. The road outside was this time shrouded in darkness. Through the glass he could hear the wind faintly howling through the telephone wires that stretched overhead. The heavens were torn with ragged clouds which seemed to race above the rooftops. Somewhere up there, behind the great grey masses that bundled across the sky there was a bright silver moon struggling to free itself. Wilson watched the battle. Maybe out there too, amongst the elements, walked the Moonlight Cat? He hoped so. He found himself fervently hoping that something or someone better, brighter and altogether more inspiring lay out there, waiting for him; waiting to show him Another Way.

Rain began to fall. The wind howled more noisily outside as the clouds started to tear themselves apart. Overcome with tiredness, Wilson slumped down upon the windowsill. He did not want to think any more; he wanted his mind to shut itself off and stop tilting crazily at every notion that crept into his brain. His eyelids lowered. The rooftops opposite flickered in light and shadow as the skies above continued in torment. As sleep finally descended upon his troubled frame, did his eyes catch at last a glimpse of a magical, shimmering creature, silvery-grey, moving with effortless grace across the skyline, over the roofs, leading off into the distance…?

The next day dawned, finding Wilson still slumbering upon the windowsill. It was late morning before the heat behind the windowpane had built up sufficiently to wake his tired body. He yawned, stretched and shook himself to prepare for the day. There was still some cat food and stale water that his mother had not finished waiting for him beneath the sink on the kitchen floor. With this breakfast inside him he wandered out into the hallway, still undecided as to what direction he should take in this new day. He stopped. The front door was wide open and the Woman of The House was out in the front garden. The decision was made. Wilson took the route that was offered to him and ran out once more into The Road.

Without hesitation he turned right, opposite to the path he had taken yesterday, hoping that the world in this direction would be a little kinder to him. The pavement stretched out in a straight line into the distance and, careful to avoid trouble, Wilson kept close alongside the base of fences and garden walls, carefully inspecting each gateway that he crossed.

A number of cars went humming past Wilson in the same direction as he was travelling. He saw that, with winking red and orange lights, they seemed to stop some way in front of him and then, the sunlight sparkling off polished metal and glass, they slowly turned and disappeared out of sight. This intrigued him. Where they went to he could not guess. Now that he thought about it, he had no idea where they all came from, either. Cars just appeared and disappeared along the road in a steady stream of colour, noise and odious smells.

Wilson hurried along impatiently, desperate to see what magic was happening some distance ahead of him. His mind was racing faster than his legs: Cars always run along roads, he thought. They come from where roads come and they go where roads go. That was what he knew; what everyone had said. So where cars disappear, so do roads... He had to see.

Another car went swishing past. This one smelt different – a scent of wet earth and shrubbery was mixed with the fumes of car exhaust. It was a dull, grey pickup with various plants waving from the back: a curious mixture, in Wilson's experience, of road and garden. He saw it stop, like all the others, not so far away now and he watched it eagerly to see what would happen to it.

He never saw the dog until too late. It was the same mongrel as yesterday – just as mean and determined now to finish the chase that had been so painfully denied him before. Focussed on the vehicle that had pulled up in front of him Wilson was unaware of the danger he was in until the snarling, vindictive cat-hater was almost on top of him. Then there was only one direction left for him to run: straight at the pickup.

The traffic lights changed and the driver of the pickup slowly put his foot down to accelerate away. As he made to negotiate the corner, some damn dog was leaping around at the back and making a lot of noise. Stupid animal! Why couldn't it see that it was senseless trying to compete with 3 litres and 16 cwt? Tyres squealed and the pickup powered its way down the next street, leaving its pursuer behind in saliva-flecked frustration. In the rear-view mirror, the dog quickly dwindled to a tiny speck. There was no other animal to be seen.

The driver was in a hurry. He had a long way to go and did not want to delay any longer, fighting his way through city traffic. Most of the plants had been sold and he was anxious to deliver the rest to a farm address some three or four hours distant.

City backstreets soon gave way to a main road which in turn led into a major highway. Within the hour, the pickup was speeding its way out of the urban sector and driving past fields, assorted crops and glasshouses. It was on its way to more mountainous, less densely-populated lands with its reduced load of cultivated plants and one unintended, and totally bewildered, passenger.

The pickup slowly bumped its way down the rough track towards its destination. Up until now, frightened by the noise, the strange movement and the rush of air over the back of his transport, Wilson had not dared attempt to reach up and look out at what was passing by. As the rhythm of movement changed, however, trees swept into view above him and rich, exciting smells quite unlike he had ever known before reached his quivering nostrils, so Wilson began to take an interest in his surroundings. The sidewall of the pickup was not so high that he could not scrabble part way up and peer over the top, his back legs on claw-tips, his front legs spread wide to support himself as the vehicle swayed over the uneven track.

What met his eyes was a world completely different to anything he had ever seen in the city. There was no tarmac road, no long straight lines nor any wall of houses that rose up all around and closed him in. No. Instead, a great expanse of rolling green fields was slowly rising and falling by him. Every few moments, trees and hedgerows danced past his incredulous eyes. The sky seemed enormous – spread above and beyond until the far distance where it seemed to blend into purple hills. Stretching round to see where his transport was heading, Wilson watched a sweep of rock slowly grow in front of him. A dark green valley was opening beneath it and the pickup was gradually closing towards its centre. As minutes ticked by, the rock face seemed to rise, unfold and reach up and back as if trying to play with the clouds. The wooded valley that flourished below was cut by a small but lively stream and, looping round to avoid its waters, there swung into view an old grey stone farmhouse and a number of glasshouses and wooden outbuildings. The rough track which the pickup was following ended there.

A heavy, five-bar gate marked the entrance to the farm. The driver negotiated this successfully and had just closed it again behind his vehicle when a riot of barking broke out. Wilson saw two large, black dogs come racing up. He caught a glimpse of slavering jaws and wicked yellow fangs and then quickly shrank back down into the shelter of the pickup. The dogs leapt around the slowly moving vehicle, barking noisily and following it as it moved towards the farmhouse. Wilson just prayed that his scent, mixed with that of the motor's exhaust and the plants that were swaying about next to him, would go undetected by the fearsome escorts outside. It seemed to. With no further interruption, the pickup passed an old, cobwebbed shack and led up to another gate. A man dressed in dark blue overalls was waiting on the other side of this. He was shouting at the dogs and waving a stick to keep them away whilst the pickup drove through and finally came to a halt.

As soon as the engine died Wilson emerged from amongst the plants and pricked up his ears. He heard the driver emerge from the cab and walk off to greet the other man. Apart from their low voices in conversation there was a surrounding quietness that somehow seemed bigger and emptier than Wilson had ever heard before. There was no sound of any dogs now so once again he reached up to look out.

The pickup was parked in front of a long, low greenhouse by the side of the main farm building. While the men were busy talking, Wilson seized his chance and jumped down from his transport. On the other side of the pickup to the men, he ran off – his eyes searching eagerly for something that offered shelter and allowed him to sit quiet whilst he took in all of this strange, new environment. A sturdy wooden barn was opposite the greenhouse. Large doors were swung open and just inside the entrance were three or four packing cases on top of which were stacked some cardboard boxes. Wilson sprang on top of the first case in a single bound and slid into cover. He settled down in the gloom beneath the doorway, thrusting a head in amongst the boxes to clear a place to rest. Safety! This place was dark, warm and had an air of undisturbed calm about it. Wilson thankfully slumped down and in seconds he had dozed off, his body tired from nervous exhaustion. Never before had sleep been so welcoming!

Most cats are by their nature independent and irrepressibly curious creatures. Nonetheless, to be whisked away from your mother, the only home you have ever known and all its familiar surroundings; to be taken off in some alien transport; threatened by loud, sharp-toothed monsters and dropped into the middle of a new and totally unknown territory is bound to shake you up a little. Many creatures you might expect by now to be scared out of their wits and looking for a hole to crawl into and hide forever. Emerging from his short slumber, Wilson was therefore understandably a little nervous, but more than this he was fascinated, absolutely captivated by all that was now in front of him. For as long as he could remember he had been preoccupied by what lay out there on the other side of the houses which walled him in – now at last he knew.

As his senses awakened, all the colours, sounds and smells of a working farm – and most of all the feeling of great, liberating space – surrounded him. It was exhilarating! He could not sit still for long – everything within him urged him to get up and go exploring.

A sound behind stopped him in his tracks. It was a very slight creaking as light footsteps passed down a wooden ladder propped up at the back of the barn. It would have been inaudible to human ears but in his current heightened awareness, to Wilson's hyperactive senses, it commanded his undivided attention. He crept out a little from the boxes, flattening down to get a good look at what was happening.

A number of cats were descending from the hayloft in the barn. In the lead came a short-haired, male tabby who looked a little heavier and older than Wilson. Behind him there came three females of varying ages and size. The middle one looked interesting: cream-coloured, sure-footed and very proud – as if she was not too pleased to be following in the footsteps of the others. Wilson was intrigued.

All four cats reached the floor of the barn and made a path to the sidewall opposite. There was a loose panel of wood here that allowed them to slip out and cross the farmyard outside. Wilson immediately launched himself after them, pausing at the loose panel to peek out and see where they were going.

Outside the farmhouse, across the strip of gravel between the two buildings, a woman was busy putting food down in a couple of porcelain bowls. The four cats kept back a little until she had finished and then, when she had walked off, they closed in on the food. The male tabby was first and turned quickly to spit and swear at the others – as if insisting that they wait until he had finished. The proud, cream female obviously did not like this and made her annoyance felt. Nonetheless she stayed in her place and did not risk a fight with her more aggressive companion. Wilson saw the male return to the food, presenting his back to the watching females.

While this little demonstration of social hierarchy was being played out, Wilson suddenly realised that he, too, was ravenously hungry. He had eaten nothing since a quick breakfast that morning and a lot of nervous energy had been burned up since then. He stared enviously at the feast that was laid out in front of him only a short distance away. He had to find some means of getting to it!

There was nothing to do but wait. He hoped desperately that the other cats were not as hungry as he and that they would not finish off all the food on offer. But he had to wait until they moved away – if he ran out now there was no way that they would tolerate an intruder pushing in and trying to eat their own food right in front of them.

The next five minutes seemed an age. Wilson remained frozen by the crack in the wooden wall, his eyes fixed on the group of cats some twenty-five yards away, his own jaws moving involuntarily as if in sympathy with those he watched. The male tabby finished first, licking his face and paws and then idly wandering off, leaving the other three alone with the food. This group seemed more fussy, investigating one bowl and then the other before deciding who was to eat where. Finally, all had their fill and then they too slowly walked off, following their leader, somewhere out of sight behind the farmhouse.

Wilson left it a couple of agonising minutes, as long as he could bear the gnawing inside of him, before he went pushing past the loose panel, out into the sunlight and over to the two bowls of half-eaten food which were calling to him.

He rapidly gobbled down the contents of the first bowl, twisting his head all around meanwhile, checking to see if anyone or anything was coming. Undisturbed, he then turned his attention to the second. He had gulped most of this down also, slowing all the time as his hunger lessened, when a voice suddenly called out – more affronted than threatening:

"Hey! Where did you come from?!"

Wilson span round in a trice. It was the cream-coloured female who had returned, quickly and quietly, to stare at him from a few yards distant.

"What are you doing? Eating our food!" again she demanded.

"You've eaten already... I was hungry," Wilson replied simply.

"Huh! I can see that... but you've got a nerve, coming in here as if you have a right to take whatever you fancy." Her voice sounded indignant but wasn't there a twinkle of humour in her expression as she said this? "How did you get here anyway?"

"It was a sort of accident. I got carried in here on the back of one of those truck things that humans use. I don't think they knew about it."

Almost imperceptibly, his companion stiffened. She lost the twinkle in her eyes. "You came by yourself? No one knows you are here?" She backed off a little. "In that case, just be careful where you go and who you see…"

"Oh." Wilson did not understand what she meant nor why she now seemed disapproving of his account. He took a few steps forward:

"What's so wrong about coming here? Why've I got to be careful??"

The cream-coloured female was a little put out by this bold newcomer blocking her way, anxiously demanding an explanation, so to gain time she promptly sat down and began to wash herself. Regaining her composure, she smiled to herself at the other's growing agitation.

"C'mon, is it so bad that I came here unannounced? Where is here, anyway? What sort of place is this?"

Wilson's concern increased as his companion completely ignored him, continuing to rearrange her coat, oblivious to his questioning. Goodness! Was her fur really so untidy on her right flank? And her hind quarters too? Her tongue pushed one way and then the other. Finally she stopped, waited for Wilson to cease his nervous prancing and then she looked him straight in the eye. The amused twinkle had returned:

"This is a very ordered place, you'll see. No strangers just walk in, by accident or otherwise. And don't think you can stop and talk to me any time you like, either. Now excuse me but I have somewhere to go and I do not wish to be delayed any longer!"

His elegant partner turned and slowly tiptoed away, her tail in the air. Wilson, frustrated, rebuffed, confused once more, stood there and watched her go.

He let a few seconds pass after his new acquaintance had disappeared from sight. Well maybe he did not understand all that she had said but at least he had a full stomach now. And if he had to be careful about what he did, that behaviour was hardly anything new for him.

He looked around. The farmhouse seemed quiet. Wilson

could detect no sign of any movement neither inside nor out. It was a large stone building, the main entrance fronting on to a driveway which also gave access to the wooden barn on one side and to a line of low greenhouses opposite. The four cats that Wilson had seen had all gone off behind the farmhouse, moving slightly uphill towards the woods that he had glimpsed from the pickup on his journey in here. That direction seemed the obvious place to start exploring.

Wilson slid along the side of the farmhouse in the dusty pathway between the farmhouse and the barn until he reached the back of the stone building. A rough, gravel backyard with a tangle of weeds in places stretched over to a wooden fence, the other side of which was lined with bushes. A few swallows wheeled and dived above him but all else in the yard seemed peaceful enough. Some old farm machine lay rusting in the middle of the open space; a wooden box-like structure stood partially hidden on its other side.

Wilson padded cautiously out towards the first patch of weeds. His slow, deliberate movement and his smoky grey colouring ensured he was not easy to spot against the gravel but a soft breeze blowing from behind his right quarters carried his scent off away and to his left so it was not too wise continuing further in that direction. He turned his gaze rightwards where the wooden fence moved round and came in closer towards the barn. A tall telegraph pole soared skywards beside the fence, supporting a number of heavy cables that swung into it from the barn and, above him, from the farmhouse. Emerging from the thatch of greenery at its base were the cats he had inadvertently followed.

The cream-coloured female was of course the first he noticed. She was accompanied by a smaller female and both were busy investigating something amongst a coil of wires at the base of the telegraph pole. Movement in the greenery behind them seemed to indicate where their companions were still occupied.

Wilson wondered whether or not to follow up on the conversation that he had started earlier. It was all very well being careful what he did and to whom he spoke, but you would never find out anything if you didn't take a few risks. He moved forward.

"Hello!" He addressed the younger of the two females who was closest.

"Aagh!" She froze in her tracks, all her hair on end. Wilson had not realised but, moving silently and coming upwind, he had completely surprised his quarry.

"Oh, I'm sorry to have frightened you. I didn't mean to give you a shock like that."

The smaller female just stared goggle-eyed at him. She was speechless. Her cooler, self-collected companion spoke for her instead.

"I don't know who you are and why you're here, but you can't come marching up here like that." The cream-coloured cat spoke severely.

"Why ever not?" Wilson smiled, but he was interrupted by an explosion of hissing further back.

The leader of this little group had returned. Stockier than Wilson and swollen with rage, he came crashing through the long grass and nettles determined to see off this intruder. Snarling viciously, he came barrelling out in a frontal assault.

Wilson did not stop to argue. He feinted left, drawing his attacker's clawing lunge to one side and then quickly darted off in the other direction, circling behind the telegraph pole and, in one leap, reaching the top of the fence. The heavier tomcat, angry and unsuccessful in his charge, skidded ponderously in the dirt, swearing and cursing at the top of his voice.

"Get away, whoever you are! Don't you ever show your face around here again! This is my territory; these are my females and if I ever catch you spreading your scent around in my yard I'll tear your insides out!!"

Wilson turned adeptly at the top of the fence and faced his

adversary. He guessed that, despite all the sound and fury, the other would not leave the females and attempt the long vault up to fight him off. He sighed. He had seen all this so many times before! One look at glaring, belligerent eyes below told him it was worthless trying to talk his way round this. A pity! The third female had appeared now and together the three looked as if they were silently resigned to this ordering of their destiny. Did they not know or care about any other ways of the world?

With the hostile tomcat spitting and fuming below, Wilson tripped lightly along the narrow line at the top of the fence and then, when an opening appeared in bramble bushes on the other side, he dropped smartly down away from the farmhouse, out of sight of his tormentor.

As soon as he hit the grass on this side of the wooden paling Wilson could smell dogs. Not again! It seemed he was yet once more running away from one danger only to rush full tilt into the jaws of another. He was on a grassy slope dotted with trees and bushes that bordered the farm and that swung around from the undulating plains below to the steep-sided valley that led up into the hills behind. Wilson hoped that, if the dogs he smelt now were the same two monsters he had seen on his way in here, then they were still round at the front of the farm and that he had enough time to make it back to the wooded valley uphill from here.

He turned and set off across the grass slopes towards the beckoning trees. As midday had now passed and the sun had warmed the plains below, the breeze that came slowly filtering up past Wilson carried a variety of farmyard scents to him and bore them further on towards the rocky outcrops that rose above the stream. With them came a whole complex of emotions. There was the ugly stench of the dogs' toilet which hung over the grass. Clearly these animals exercised here often. The smell of the cats from the other side of the fence was clearly discernible too – they were so near yet so far from him. He was saddened by this. He so wanted to meet and to mix with them, to understand more of their world and have them understand more of his. There were other strange odours he could pick up in the wind also, unknown aromas that aroused his interest and excited his sense of adventure. They were the signature of strange animals and plants that he could only guess at.

He turned all these conflicts over in his mind as he followed the hillside round towards the trees: He accepted his father's advice that he had to find his own way, that only he could push back the boundaries of his own ignorance, but were there nowhere to be found a few more welcoming and understanding voices? Surely there were other cats somewhere that were not tied down by their own jealousies, and that shared his desire to go out, higher and further, and follow the Moonlight Cat wherever He may lead? He had never before seen open field and distant woods until now but did not such things call to them the same as they called to him?

And the valley he was now approaching looked absolutely fascinating. It was a cats' playground of trees, bushes and bubbling waters that came splashing down from rocks somewhere above. His spirits rose at the sight of it all: previous to this his only knowledge of the wonders of nature had been what had been allowed to flower in a collection of city back gardens. This profusion of space, colour and form in front of him was, in contrast, much greater, much grander, and thick with the promise of adventure. It was mesmerising. He could scarcely take it all in but he knew instinctively that the way to a richer, fuller life that he had always dreamed about led in this direction. It was like looking at the doorway to a greater destiny.

At the same time as these sensations were sweeping over him, the pungent scent of approaching danger assailed his nostrils. Dogs were coming. The two villainous black hounds from the farm had appeared downwind and they were scouring the hillside below looking for trouble. It would not be long before they gave up chasing false leads, picked up Wilson's trail and then followed it straight to him.

Wilson quickly considered his options for escape. His nearest refuge was a tree and some bushes a little way ahead. Beyond that, other trees grew in thicker profusion in the wood beside the stream. Alternatively he could make a quick dash across the grass to the fence which had accompanied him and the farmyard and greenhouses that it protected on the other side.

Just as he was gauging the distances involved, he noticed a sudden frenzy of activity behind him. The dogs were chasing some small, brown creature across the hillside. Wilson had never seen a rabbit before so he had no idea what it was that was jinking frantically through the grass. All he could make out were two ferocious beasts closing in with murderous intent on some poor, doomed animal.

Wilson did not want to look. Try as it might, the panic-stricken creature could not find a way to safety past its two savage pursuers. It twisted and turned with increasing desperation to avoid snapping and plunging jaws. Finally, with a triumphant wrench, one dog threw his head back and flung the helpless rabbit cartwheeling into the air, before leaping upward and catching it again with a vicious crunch of its teeth. The rabbit's faint, high-pitched scream clawed at Wilson's heart. It seemed to pierce his soul.

Trembling, he turned and made his way carefully towards the nearest tree. With the two brutes below worrying over the remains of the poor rabbit he knew he now had plenty of time to reach safety. Circling round behind some bushes he concealed himself and watched the hounds as they finished their grisly task. He felt rising within him a sense of anger, the sort of unreasoning hatred of dogs that his father had earlier spoken of. As he watched, he saw them eventually leave the bloodied carcass and return to patrolling the hillside. A few moments later he heard them growl in anticipation as they picked up another fresh scent:

his own. The two dogs bounded menacingly upslope towards him and Wilson felt himself involuntarily baring his teeth and snarling silently at their approach. With a swish of his tail, he stole away to the base of the tree and swiftly climbed its trunk. He soon reached the first of a number of spreading boughs and, declining to go higher, he padded along a few steps and then flattened down against the branch, partially hidden, to watch his trackers.

He did not have long to wait. They soon came searching around, barking and howling in annoyance when they lost the trail below. One raised his head and bellowed out his frustration and Wilson saw himself looking down upon bloodshot eyes and long lines of wicked, yellow fangs. Again, his instinctive reaction was to curl back his own lips and spit angrily in reply. The dogs' response was to go mad with fury – roaring, howling, twisting and thrashing about the tree trunk: here was their quarry, incitingly close but just out of reach. No matter how they leaped and gnashed the air, they could get no satisfaction. Eventually, realising how futile it was tiring themselves out in this way, they stopped their restless onslaught.

Snarling viciously, one swore in a guttural, barely understandable accent: "We'll get you! No one escapes. Nothing moves here that we don't hunt down sooner or later. We'll rip you apart..."

With that, the two dogs quietened down and retreated a little way off to rest. His vision partly obscured by the leaves, Wilson saw them flop down hiding on the other side of the bushes, their heads lowered but their eyes and ears nonetheless pricked and turned in his direction. They were not fooling anyone!

Although confronted by the biggest and undoubtedly the most dangerous dogs he had ever seen in his life, and despite trembling like the leaves that now surrounded him, Wilson nonetheless kept a clear head and he was reasonably confident that he could keep himself out of harm's way. If he now climbed a little higher in this tree he was sure he could pass into the branches of another, and then through that he could get access to the wood where the trees and undergrowth grew too close for other animals much larger than himself to move with freedom.

He moved silently and sure-footedly through the tree and then boldly, rather than leap and struggle through the myriad of interlocking twigs and branches, he decided to drop lightly to the ground and sprint quickly to the next cover. It was ridiculously easy. The dogs were slow to pick up his initial movement amongst the leaves and so they were unable to stop him when he made his dash across the open.

Wilson now entered a world of gloom and greenery where he could choose to move alternately up trees or through and under bushes. With his enemies unable to follow here he was safe from assault for the time being, so he pranced and pounced along until finally he found his way blocked by rushing waters. The stream was not great in size but it came scattering downslope, splashing violently. Since he had no desire to get a soaking, he followed it downhill as best he could until it offered a better place to cross.

This was a paradise for Wilson. Full of sparkle and life, the stream leapt down over steps in the bank, from pools where insects and butterflies fluttered, past chattering rapids and then on swirling round bends where the mountainside closed in. Spongy moss and long creepers clung to the sides, trees hung low in places and all manner of small birds zipped across the waters as Wilson emerged first from behind one clump of green, then another.

Time quickly passed in this wonderland. Wilson explored one side of the stream and then – crossing by a fallen log – he entered the other, enjoying the freedom and variety of challenges offered throughout the wood. Finally he settled down in a dry patch beneath a bush and rested. It had been a long day. His mind reeled with images of urban streets; of countryside flashing past;

of beautiful felines, terrifying hounds and, ultimately, of waving branches and sunbeams filtered green by the canopy of leaves. He had come through an amazing series of experiences and, indeed, he was still struggling to make sense of it all. But slowly, fitfully, he let it all slip from his consciousness and he drifted off at last into a welcoming sleep.

He woke with a start. It was pitch black around and, rousing himself for the first time in the open air and in a strange new place, it took him a few seconds to realise where he was. Then, with a leap in his heart, it all became crystal clear: he was in the wood!

Wilson had been born and raised as a domestic animal in a terraced house in the city but it said much for his strength of character – and his feline inheritance – that awakening for the first time in the wild in total darkness he nonetheless felt completely at ease, invigorated even. The call of the wild was in his blood which meant that this was not the time any longer for dozing on some city sofa, but he must get out and about and see what the night offered.

The air was very heavy, however, and there was a threatening rumble of thunder in the distance. Lights flickered high in the sky above the trees and, inexperienced though he still was, he knew that a rainstorm would not be long in coming. Perhaps, he thought, it might be wise to look around for some shelter before the downpour began.

With eyes widened to pick up the faintest glimmer beneath the trees, Wilson made his way slowly downhill. A plan was beginning to form in his mind: rather than take up the option to explore his present surroundings, he was drawn to a place that offered shelter *and* the possibility of easy food and another liaison with the female that fascinated him: It was the farm on the other side of the fence below.

Large, ominous drops of rain had just started to fall when he reached the outskirts of the wood. Somewhere over in the blackness to his side he could hear the stream chattering away, but before him lay a dark swathe of open hillside that swooped away downslope into the gloom to where he knew a line of bushes and the occasional tree marked where the wooden fence ran.

There was suddenly a flash of lightning, a deafening clap of thunder and then the rain started in earnest. The cloudburst quickly soaked the leaves above him and came down noisily pattering all around. Unsettled by this rude invasion, Wilson hunched up his fur and hurried out into the open, heading for the distant farm.

Almost as soon as he had done so, he knew he had made a mistake. Why had he not taken greater care before setting out from shelter? Despite being difficult to see in this darkness, and with the heavens opening above, two sinister watchdogs had been lying in wait for him. From his scent, which had been carried down on the cooling mountain air, they knew he was close by, and for these experienced hunters it was just a question of waiting until their quarry broke cover. They closed in with terrifying suddenness. One came at him from behind his left quarter; the other a little further back from somewhere near the stream. Being chased on both sides, there was no option to turn and try and make it back to the trees so Wilson's only hope now was to accelerate downslope as fast as his strength would last and trust to finding some sort of escape below.

Help! This was utter madness – something from out of his worst nightmare: He found himself racing crazily through the darkness with the rain pouring out of the sky, his heart pounding, his mind screaming and with nowhere in front of him to go.

Through the drenching rain, Wilson could hear his pursuers behind galloping ever closer. Large paws were pounding and splashing through mud and over heath; fearful muzzles hung open, panting and slobbering for the kill. And where to go?? The grassy slope continued to roll away into the night with no promise of any refuge. Rapidly tiring, the hopelessness of his situation threatened to overwhelm his brain in panic. Wilson sensed he only had a few seconds remaining before he was lost. Desperately, he threw his body into a ninety-degree turn, veering rightwards and across the path of one of his attackers. He narrowly evaded the heaving pounce of huge jaws and, whilst larger bodies skidded to readjust their line, he started off away in the direction of the stream he knew must be close.

Not quite knowing what he would do, he started sliding down in a gully towards the swollen waters as the hounds came at him again. This time he found it very soft and muddy underfoot and, with the rain sluicing down and the stream spraying everywhere, his lighter weight meant it was much easier for him to manoeuvre here than it was for his heavier assailants. Rocks miraculously appeared in the silvery, translucent light of rushing waters and, despite the soaking, he managed to keep his feet and gain the other side of the stream. Adrenalin searing through his veins, he bounded up the loose, steep-sided slope that confronted him on the other side and then he was free, atop the gorge with his terrifying pursuers still below, floundering amongst the soft earth and water.

There was no time to rest. Running exhausted but less panic-stricken now, he set off to cover the remaining distance to the farm. Forcing his brain to calm down and think rationally, he figured that there would be no way his trackers could smell him out in this downpour. Once they had lost sight of him in the darkness, he was safe. Wilson kept going until he was sure that the night had swallowed him up. Then, thankfully, he relaxed to a slow walk.

Minutes later, looming out of the night, Wilson saw the dark shape of the fence standing tall on the skyline back on the other side of the gully. He had only to cross the stream once more and scale the wooden palings to reach his destination. This time he checked very carefully that the dogs were nowhere close. Then he crept down the bank and, working out carefully the safest place to cross, with a rush and a leap he splashed his way over. Somewhat bedraggled after contending with both stream and storm, Wilson finally got to the fence with just enough strength left to climb up and reach the top. He was certain that no other cat would be out in these awful conditions so it was just a matter now of getting out of the rain, shaking himself dry and trying to recover from his ordeal.

It was another hour before the storm passed. Rainclouds finally scudded clear of the mountaintop and a new moon emerged in the lightening skies to look down on the farm below. Nothing moved in the cool, damp, early morning breeze. Then a faint, silver-grey shadow seemed to detach itself from beneath the rusting metal hulk of some strange agricultural machine and hover, shimmering in the steamy air. As silently as it appeared, it vanished.

"Mummy, Mummy, I've just seen the Moonlight Cat!" a tiny kitten turned excitedly to its mother in the hayloft.

"Hush, my dear, come back over here and go to sleep. There's nothing outside in this rainstorm."

"No, Mummy, come and see! It's almost stopped now and the moon is out and... and you said that's when you can see the Moonlight Cat... and THERE HE IS AGAIN!!!"

Beside himself in excitement, he awoke his brother and sisters and even his aunts came over to have a look. A line of young and old faces peered out of the hayloft into the dawn.

"I can't see anything! Where you looking?"

"Down there by that tractor thing."

"What? Down where old Fabio used to live?"

"It's too dark... I can't see a thing over there."

"What's a Moonlight Cat doing over there anyway?"

"Just wait, you'll see... THERE!!! Didn't I say!!"

Everyone fell silent. The backyard glistened in the wet, hazy dawn light and there, undoubtedly, floating over one of the distant puddles moved a distinctly feline shape. It made no noise nor caused the faintest ripple in the water-logged surface. Was it the Moonlight Cat?

The kittens were convinced:

"It's him! It's him!"

"He's gone again."

"But he'll be back, you see."

"Not if he crosses the back fence like that other cat, he won't."

"Who says? He will if it's the Moonlight Cat. He goes wherever he will and He shows us The Way."

"Well you are not going *that* way, whatever He shows you!" Their mother gathered them together and tried to quieten them down. "Listen to what your aunt told you yesterday: those dogs killed another poor cat yesterday so just you keep away from there."

"Who was it?"

"We don't know. A visitor. I only saw him on the top of the fence and then I heard the dogs… Now no more questions. Get back to sleep all of you!"

Wilson sniffed the air. He had learnt a lot in a short time. The farmyard was still dark and gloomy in the early morning and although the oppressive storm-laden air had passed he was not going to assume it was safe to go out. He carefully sidestepped some puddles that blocked his way and prowled round to investigate the low wooden box-like structure that stood close by his hiding place. He stopped and sniffed again. Despite being washed clean by the rain, a faint smell of cats lingered here. All senses alert, he very gingerly inched forward. Noiselessly, he checked all around and about the wooden shelter before approaching its entrance. There was neither scent nor sign of any creature inside, yet there was some presence here – he could *feel* it.

"Welcome, stranger! Come on in."

Wilson nearly jumped out of his skin. The voice came whispering out totally unexpectedly.

"Have no fear, my son, my brother. Come in."

Very cautiously, Wilson rounded the timber sidewall and looked through the opening. In the heavy shadow he could just make out an old, tortoiseshell cat with twinkling eyes sitting quietly in the middle of the straw-covered interior.

"I… I'm sorry. I didn't think anyone was here…" he stuttered. He couldn't understand why for the life of him he had not smelt nor seen any trace of this animal from the outside.

"That's alright. Don't worry. Come in and dry yourself off. You must be soaked after having been out there all night." The eyes seemed to shine even brighter as he spoke.

Despite the eeriness of this introduction, Wilson felt no fear. His host spoke faintly but with warmth and directness so he did as he was bade. He turned round and settled in the straw. It was good to feel the dry fibres drain the last of the moisture from his fur.

The old cat watched him. "You have met the hounds outside, then…" It was more of a statement than a question.

Wilson started. He felt the anger, fear and frustration rise within him. "I've met them all right! Mindless killers they are," he spat it out. "I hate 'em!"

His older companion smiled at him. "I understand your pain. You have struggled much against these and others, I see."

"Why are they all out to get me?" Wilson asked plaintively. "It's not just the dogs, though they are the worst. Most cats I've met seem to want to fight me too…" He looked cautiously at his new acquaintance as he said this. Sensing no hostile reaction he continued: "All I've ever wanted to do is explore a little but no sooner do I find somewhere new than I also find some monster trying to kill me! It's not fair! Why is it all so difficult?"

Wilson's notion of injustice was affronted; and now that he

was for the first time in the presence of someone who he felt would listen, a great wave of emotion began to break over him. "I only wanted to find the Way of the Moonlight Cat..." his voice began to shake.

"Tush!" the older cat sniffed, though he looked down upon Wilson kindly. "Did the Moonlight Cat say it would be easy? It isn't. Life is neither fair nor unfair; it is neither easy nor difficult. You are just not seeing it the right way. These events are not major obstacles in your life. They are opportunities! There is no malicious power in the universe that is set out to frustrate you. What you see as difficulties are there for your benefit; to stimulate your growth. It is for you to use your talents to overcome these little trials on Your Way. Remember – you are just a Shadow of the Moonlight Cat."

"My growth? Those dogs out there trying to kill me are for my benefit?" It did not make sense to Wilson. Just thinking about how close he had come to being caught by them caused his blood to rise again. "I hate 'em!" He repeated himself vehemently.

"Do not hate." His companion rebuked him. "Hatred acts as a poison to your spirit: rise above it. The Moonlight Cat does not hate. You must understand that *they simply do not Know*. These poor creatures have only one destiny – to roar and rage at all that life has given them. They know not how to transcend this level. So forgive them their tirades: all that energy spent in fury and fear."

"Fear?" This was something new. "*They* are afraid?"

"Yes! They fear the loss of power, of their tiny kingdoms. They do not know how precious little they really have, and how much more they could have if only they could open their eyes and *see*! But you can see. You must. See *all* the world and your part in it. Keep looking beyond: at all that lives and loves and moves on this Earth. Keep working at it and one day you will walk amongst them without fear. They will touch you not. They will neither injure your body nor scar your soul. You will walk unharmed like the Moonlight Cat with tread so light it barely touches the ground. You will walk at night between the stars and in the day you will float above the grass. Remember whose Shadow you are. Have faith and you can do it all!"

Wilson gaped in amazement. The older cat's voice was faint and weak but he spoke with a simplicity and authority that was utterly convincing.

"You... you are the Moonlight Cat...?"

Another kindly smile. The eyes twinkled again: "My son, my son, I was much like you when I was young. I understood so little and yet wanted to know so much. I too set out to follow the Way of the Moonlight Cat. Everywhere I searched I seemed to get no closer and yet all the time I never knew that I was walking precisely in His footsteps. So close... so close, but I could never see!" He paused. "And you, my brother? Have *you* seen Him? Do you know His Way?"

"N... no... I know nothing..." Wilson felt very humble.

"But you have followed Him far closer than I! I see it all in your face, my son. Have you not already travelled great distances? Have you not already twice outrun the hounds? None other than the Moonlight Cat has done these things. Certainly not I, nor any other cat here. Yet you... you walk in His Shadow."

"But how do you know? How can you tell? And how can *I* come to know the right Way?"

"Look inside yourself and you will find all that you need to succeed. You must first take the journey inward before you can find the route outside. You must aspire to perfection, just as the Moonlight Cat is perfect; to follow His Way; in His footsteps. Do not let anything deflect you from this Path. The deeper you go, the further you look, the more you will see that we are all part of the same Plan. Those you now perceive as enemies you will come to understand as an essential part of your destiny. They are to help you on your Way. And have faith: you *can* succeed.

"But I see you are cold and very tired now. You have been

through a lot recently. Lie down, rest and get warm again. There is plenty of time to think over these things and talk again in the future. Now you should sleep..."

It was impossible to resist: the old cat's manner was quietly hypnotic. Wilson felt reassured, welcome, secure. He curled round in the straw and quickly dozed off.

He could only have slept for a few minutes but the difference Wilson felt when he awoke was immense. It was as if he had been recharged with incredible energy; as if electricity powered through his body, making him glow from tip to tail. Strong, bright, confident, he leapt up and could not wait to get started on the day.

First and most of all, he wanted to thank his host for all his kindness. He had helped lift a great load which had been oppressing him for so long. But where was his mentor? There was now no one else in the shelter. The old cat had quietly stolen away whilst Wilson was asleep.

Meanwhile, Wilson's stomach complained. He was hungry! Well, the old cat had said that they would talk later so perhaps it was time now to attend to more urgent matters. Outside the wooden shelter, the morning air was steaming in the sun where the shadows had shortened over the water-soaked yard. Wilson glided out and quickly looked round. There was nothing to delay him here so he slid off to investigate the farmhouse and any meal that might be available.

Used to the way of humans, Wilson guessed he had a little time still before they got up and moved about the house. Since any food left outside would have long ago been washed away in the downpour his only hope for a quick feast was to get in and raid the kitchen.

In the event, it was ridiculously easy. A window close by the back door was fitted with horizontal glass slats, much like he had seen before in the city terraces. Sitting on the dustbin outside, he had inserted a paw and levered the slats up and open. A tight squeeze and he was in. There was an interesting-looking packet standing on the floor beneath the kitchen sink and from its half-opened top he could smell breakfast. Knocking the packet over ensured some of its contents spilled out over the floor and Wilson took no time in devouring all of this. With his stomach now content, he toyed with the idea of sniffing further around inside the house, but caution prevailed and so he decided to leave as quickly and quietly by the same route as he had entered.

Sunlight was mirroring off the glass slats as he squeezed himself out so there was a split-second delay before he took in that there was another cat opposite, some distance away from the farmhouse. Wilson sank down on top of the dustbin lid and made himself small, relying on the contrasting shadow and sunlight to break up his shape, making him difficult to spot. At the same time, squinting hard, he tried to figure out which cat it was on the other side of the yard and whether or not it had noticed anything.

He relaxed. It was the youngest of the three females he had seen the day before and no sooner had he ascertained this than she had run off out of sight around the corner. Whether she had seen him or not he could not say but the coast was now clear for him to slip away unmolested.

He set off, but where to go? Where was *his* Way? He paused. Seeing the young cat again reminded Wilson that there was something, or rather someone, that was missing in his life. It was suddenly blindingly obvious in which direction he should go now. It had been obvious from the moment he had first seen her, if only he would accept it. He needed to find the cream-coloured female.

"Pippa! Whatever is the matter with you?"

The young cat had appeared trembling all over, barely able to move and with eyes wide in shock or awe or something. Her older friend was instantly concerned.

"I... I... think I've just seen the Moonlight Cat..."

"Oh Pippa... do make sense!" her worldly-wise companion complained.

"No... no... the kittens were right. I saw Him," the younger one blurted out. "Yes, I know what you think, Madeleine. You've got everything so together; you are so confident and nothing ever shakes you. But I saw Him just like the kittens did and there's no other explanation. He just appeared and then melted away – like that! I... I was down by the back door of the farmhouse and honestly there was no one there, not anyone remotely near. And then this bright light seemed to shine at me – bright as anything. When the light went, there He was... looking at me... looking straight through me. I was mortified. I... I couldn't believe it. And then He just seemed to vanish again – into thin air." Pippa burst into tears. The whole experience had been emotionally devastating for her.

"There now, cousin, don't get yourself so upset. If it was Him, then why are you crying?"

"It was... it was... it was Him," burbled the younger cat. She was crying freely with none of her friend's composure.

"Yes, yes, of course. I believe you," comforted Madeleine. Really she did not know whether to believe her or not; but whatever had happened, whatever her younger, more impressionable relative had seen, it had clearly shaken her to the core. "Come over here and lie down. You've had a shock, haven't you? Come here where it is quiet and warm and rest yourself, first of all. You need a little time to recover, don't you? There... that's better..."

Madeleine worried over her cousin and made sure that she felt secure and comfortable in the hayloft – *and* that she was settled down some distance away from the barn end where it overlooked the backyard. Sitting reassuringly close by, she waited for her young companion's body to stop trembling before she made any hint of a move. Then, once the other's breathing had returned to a steady, less-excited rhythm, Madeleine judged she could risk leaving her. She slowly rose and padded off to the ladder that descended down to the barn below.

Moments later, Madeleine peeked out from behind the big barn doors. She knew it was a risk, going out without Duke's permission, but this was an emergency and anyway she wanted to show him that he could not always have it his own way. He was getting insufferable.

Careful to check left and right first, she started to cross over to the farmhouse with the idea of following the path round to the back door, but then a loud voice roared out to stop her. It was Duke, the tomcat.

"Hey! Waddya think you're doing?" He came pounding over. "Who told you to go out prowling around when you're supposed to be inside with all the others?"

Madeleine held her head up. "No one *told* me. Why should anyone tell me? Why should *you* tell me what I can or cannot do? I've decided to go out by myself and it's time you left me alone and let me lead my own life."

Duke immediately lost his temper. There was no way he could match the articulate way she expressed her independence except by resort to brute strength. He flew at her, enraged.

The first blow knocked her over backwards and she could only avoid more by retreating rapidly to the safety of the barn. She vaulted up on top of the packing cases and turned to face her heavier opponent below.

"You brute! You beast! I've told you: leave me alone! Let me be! What gives you the right to keep knocking us about like this?"

Duke was spitting and swearing. He did not attempt to answer any of her questions. "Don't you leave here, gettit? Don't you leave here again unless you want more of that." He bared his teeth and snarled menacingly. "I'm the one who gives the orders around here and don't you *ever* forget it!"

Madeleine spat at him but she did not move. Duke glared back. Confident then that this challenge to his superiority had been forcibly overcome, he gradually withdrew. He turned arrogantly, sauntered out into the sunshine and flopped down, his muscles flexing, his tail twitching, his ego swollen.

Madeleine fumed. She could tell by his idle sprawl that he had one eye fixed on the barn door. There was no escape there. She climbed down and moved into the darkness on the other side of the interior. She was furious, getting angrier by the second. How dare he! There was no way she could accept him trampling all over her. She did not care – she had to get out! But thinking and doing are two different things: she hovered beside the loose wooden panel, too frightened to move just yet. She knew full well the consequences if she slipped out now behind his back. Tears of frustration welled up within her. What hurt most of all was that she was contemplating going out in search of an ideal, a phantom, a Moonlight Cat. And that big, brutish, unfeeling ogre was slowly, day-by-day, beating any such idealism out of her. No! It was too much! She could not let him do it any more. With a swish of her tail she pushed aside the panel and hopped out.

Straight as an arrow, she darted across to the farmhouse, praying that Duke would not look behind him. Fear lending her speed, she made the corner and turned, breathless but out of sight now from the barn doors. Phew! Her heart was thumping crazily. She leaned up against the back wall for support.

It took her a few seconds to recover, then she cautiously moved forward, her mind trying to focus on what she had come for, though her insides were still in turmoil. She had only gone a few yards when suddenly she froze, stiff legged, rigid as ice. She felt her eyes grow big, round and saucer-like. She could not believe it: A grey, feline shadow had suddenly, magically, detached itself from the wall and it stood there silently in front of her, blocking her way.

"Hello!" The Shadow smiled.

The spell was broken. Madeleine let out a great sigh.

"My goodness! Don't *do* that!"

"Oh sorry! Have I given you a shock again?"

"A shock! I almost died! I thought for a moment you were the... you were... Wait a minute! I... I thought you were dead! Didn't those dogs... er... get you yesterday?" She struggled and failed to regain her composure.

The Shadow smiled again, broader this time: "No, they didn't. But how did you know that they tried?"

"They kill anything that moves over there," she said with a shudder. "They've killed at least two cats that I know of – the last one was old Fabio, only a week ago – and then... and then we heard them making the same awful noise again yesterday after you went over the fence."

"Well they are vicious hounds, right enough, but it's easy to get away from them amongst the trees." His face changed, becoming more introspective, peaceful: "The woods are beautiful. It is a wonderful place over there, did you know?"

He said it so simply, unpretentiously, it reached out and touched her heart.

Madeleine gulped. "No... no... I've never been..." She really was having trouble trying to keep control of the situation. He was so unlike any tomcat she had ever met before.

Gently, shyly, the Shadow asked: "Why don't you come and see? You'll never believe the colour, the sheer magic of the place. It's like walking in paradise. I promise you, you will be safe there."

Madeleine was captivated. Something cried within her. This cat was talking to her in a language she had never heard before. But he was suggesting something outrageous. What on Earth was happening?

Wilson waited patiently. "Will you come?"

Large, soft, peaceful eyes were looking at her. Madeleine

considered the alternative.

"Yes! C'mon, let's go right away!" It was easy to decide.

Wilson led the way. He paused on top of the fence to sniff the air, then – assured that no threat of dogs was near – he dropped down beside the gully below. Choosing to avoid the open grassy slopes, he escorted his new friend along the course of the meandering stream towards the waiting woods.

The two cats entered their wonderland. The valley had been washed clean by the storm overnight and, illuminated now by the bright, clear, morning sunlight, the world below the trees was endlessly fascinating. They chased, they climbed, they took it in turns to hide and pounce out on one another. Brought together from very different backgrounds, these two could both share in the delight of discovering more about each other and about this totally new environment. They revelled in the liberation from their past confines and in the promise of all that this entrancing place offered. The bond between them grew.

They knew, of course, that it was only a matter of time before the ferocious guardians of the mountainside made another appearance. The two cats took to playing on the eastern fringes of the wood where the warm breeze, rising during the day from the farmlands below, would bring an early warning of their approach, plus there was an uninterrupted view over the grassy slopes for some distance.

In the event, they heard them first. A faint barking rose from the bushes bordering the fence a long way over to their left. Then Wilson saw them bobbing and bounding their way upslope as they slowly climbed on a rising line towards their valley: two dark, powerful animals – one slightly younger and lighter in weight than the other but both concentrating intently, with noses down, following whatever scent drew their attention.

Confident that he was undetected and with plenty of time still before the hounds drew near, Wilson sat calmly watching the scene below with a mixture of feelings. He could imagine the point of view of all the cats back in the city, and that of his father, seeing these animals zigzagging over the turf in the inimitable style of two committed hunters: they would react with instinctive fear and hatred. If given time to think any more, they would probably pour scorn on the way these beasts seem to be led by the nose – heads down, eyes almost unseeing, their backs rising and falling in waves. Wilson realised that he, too, would be easily drawn into ridiculing these hounds – the way they thought, sounded and moved. They were completely alien creatures from a feline point of view. If he had stayed in the city, in the company of the other cats, he knew that that was exactly what he would have grown up thinking. In fact, until yesterday it was precisely such instinctive reactions that *were* drawn out of him in his encounter with those two beasts. And yet now, having spoken with that old tortoiseshell cat, he could begin to see another way of looking at them. They were a part of this mountainside – as tied to it, indeed just as inalterably, as these trees all around. They moved over and plundered its surface in a sort of fearful harmony with the environment. Wilson could even begin to appreciate how their noses drove them, how their huge muscles operated to propel them forward and how they worked perfectly together – two creatures so obviously of the same pack. They were completely in tune with their surroundings here and, no matter how murderously they functioned, these two killers played an integral part in the story of this mountain.

These musings did not mean, however, that Wilson was entirely indifferent to the dogs' rapid approach. It was time to retreat! Madeleine was playing nearby, just on the other side of a couple of bushes. He called to her.

"C'mon, let's go. We don't want them to get any closer!"

Madeleine ran across as Wilson turned away but, as she bounded between the two bushes, she suddenly gave a scream and collapsed amongst the brambles.

Wilson quickly came to her side: "What's the matter, what have you done?"

Tangled up amongst the leaves and thorns beneath the bush, Madeleine was shaking one foot in pain and desperation. "It hurts! It hurts! Get me loose – quick!"

Wound around her forefoot and snaking in and out amongst the brambles was a line of old, rusty barbed wire. With rising alarm, Madeleine tried to pull free but, as she did so, the barb that was still embedded in her foot tore deeper. With another small cry she collapsed again. "Help me, help me! Please! They'll find me..." She cast a terrified look over her shoulder at the two hounds getting nearer by the minute.

"Don't move! They haven't seen us yet and they can't smell anything from that direction... let me see here." Wilson tried to release her paw from the cruel splinter that held her.

Concentrating hard, he tried to pull back the offending piece of wire with his teeth. Madeleine flinched and suffered silently from the pain that went shooting up her foreleg but thankfully the barb came out. With Wilson holding on tightly to the rusty wire with his teeth, she carefully lifted her paw free. But now time was running out – with the dogs so close there was no way the two of them could run safely for the cover of the trees – certainly Madeleine would never make it with her leg in so much pain. She understood the situation immediately.

"Don't leave me alone! They'll kill me...!" She looked at Wilson with fear in her eyes.

Wilson bent down and nuzzled her fondly. "I *am* going to have to leave you... but they'll not find you, I promise. Just lie still here and I'll draw them off. Give it plenty of time for them to completely disappear and then you can come out." He smiled at her gently. "Do you think you can make it back to the farm on your own OK? I'll keep those dogs with me so I shan't come back..."

Madeleine nodded in silence. The pain; the fear; his beauty: it brought tears to her eyes.

Wilson licked her face. "Have faith. It's going to be all right..."

With that, he crept out of the bushes. His body low, ears flat back, he snaked sinuously amongst the hummocky grass, moving purposefully upslope towards the steeper ground. Twenty yards off, it seemed impossible that the two hunters could not see him but they were focussing intently still on what was at a nose length away. With every second that passed, meanwhile, Wilson slunk further uphill and further from the bushes where Madeleine lay. He floated over the slopes like a grey shadow in the breeze then, boldly, arrogantly, he stood up straight, swished his tail and sprayed his scent over the stony mountainside.

Both dogs looked up, howled and bounded as one in his direction. The race was on!

This time, because it was Wilson who had chosen to enter battle and he was not now the unsuspecting victim as in all past conflicts, he felt entirely more confident about what he was doing. He was not fleeing in blind panic, trying frantically to find a way out of a desperate situation not of his choosing. On this occasion, he started with a clear head and could thus try and keep the initiative in whatever followed.

Not that it was going to be at all easy with these two ferocious killers panting after him – he headed directly upwards, choosing the steepest line available, guessing correctly that these two large, powerful beasts would not quickly overhaul him in this terrain. The higher they climbed, the more grass and heather gave way to stony soil and now Wilson could hold his own in the chase as heavier canine feet began to slip and slide a little.

Seeing their foe hovering tantalisingly close, but getting no closer, the two hounds began to growl with frustration – their jaws hanging open, slavering in rage. They began snarling and barking in fury, trying to strike fear into their quarry – fear that would normally drain the strength and paralyse the brain of any other poor creature they were chasing. Wilson, however, remained coolly in command – aloof from their predictable attempts to encumber him and seize control of events. He veered off to the left now, on a diagonal line up the mountain following a narrow rabbit track towards a rocky outcrop above. Although at a shallower angle, the track was still not wide enough for the dogs to really power away and accelerate regardless of their footholds. Wilson held to his lead.

The rapid climb was beginning to exhaust him, but still he remained unflustered and clear in his objective: the rock tower ahead which stood proud against the skyline. The gradient slackened a little over the last few yards he covered and it was littered with stones and boulders. He raced on, sensing the possibility of trying something different here. Rounding the base of the tower, he saw the mountain fall away steeply on the other side – down towards the stream and trees below. This was the place, he decided: a few yards further and he could leap up on top of a boulder and await his pursuers.

The two hunters came thundering after him, over the stones and fallen blocks, up to the tower and round the corner on the narrow path. The younger, slightly smaller one appeared first, then the heavier, angrier one – jaws open, fangs bared, dripping with saliva.

Neither of them saw it coming. Wilson launched his attack by soaring into the air, clearing the first dog from above, hitting the path all four feet together and springing forward again in one full, flowing movement to crash into the second hound at neck height, just above his right shoulder.

The force of colliding with this enormous monster nearly bounced him off, but Wilson sank all his claws in and bit deeply into the rolls of fur around the dog's neck. Even so, at the speed at which they came together, Wilson's rear legs spiralled across the other's back, scouring long marks in the black hide. Adjusting his grip, he fastened on tight, bracing himself for the inevitable explosion. The reaction of the hound was instinctive – he reared, throwing his head up and back, gnashing the air furiously, trying to get a hold on this panther which had struck him from nowhere. But the path was too narrow for such a large animal that was twisting and trying to change direction at speed. Roaring and bucking in anger, one back leg slipped away from under him. Off balance now, with the cat from hell hanging on and pulling him over, the hound's large body slewed round off the path and empty space opened up beneath him. Despite urgent scrabbling to regain his footing, and with his head still unthinkingly turning and snapping at his assailant, the dog keeled over and started sliding away.

Wilson let go and leapt clear to save himself. Lithe and athletic, he managed with little difficulty to claw on to some rocks and hold his weight. However, the other much heavier animal was now sliding and bouncing down, half on his side, his back legs pawing the air. He was unable to stop himself. The momentum began to build up in the fall, and within seconds there was no escape possible. He went crashing down faster and faster, bringing earth and stones down with him, thumping with ever-increasing force against rock and boulder. It was awful to watch. There was a long drop, another bone-crunching smack, and the stricken hound went spinning, cartwheeling into the gully. He finally came to rest with a sickening jolt that sent up a small cloud of dirt, dust and spray from the stream-filled course below. A faint whimper filtered up on the rising air, but there was no movement in the large, dust-covered body.

Wilson stood up on the narrow path and faced the other hound. He waited.

Something stopped the other from rushing into an instinctive attack. Was it the narrow footing; the sight of his brother plunging out of sight over the mountain's edge; the faint sound of death below, or was it the unnerving calm and equilibrium of his adversary before him? The second dog did not move. He let out a whine. He was a creature of the pack and his mind was in trauma. His leader, his brother had been lost.

The grey cat stepped quietly aside. It was as if he was saying: "Go now. Go and attend to your brother, whatever good that may do for him. Go and let there be an end to this. No more fighting. We are equal." No words were uttered but this cat's slow, deliberate movement was as eloquent a statement as any could be.

The younger dog understood. He moved off. With lowered head, he turned back along the rabbit path and, where he could, picked his way down as steeply as he dared heading in the direction of the gully where the other dog lay. Wilson watched him go silently, sombrely. It was all over.

Madeleine lay motionless, her heart in her mouth, watching Wilson glide away from her. Although she was still frightened, this beautiful animal was so direct, honest and uncomplicated that he inspired her complete trust. She waited quietly for him to work his magic.

The two vicious hunters never discovered her position. As if pulled by the same leash, they suddenly went racing off above her, howling and baying, and she could hear their angry cries growing ever more distant.

After a few minutes, she judged it safe enough to try and stand up. Rising painfully from amongst the tangle of leaves and brambles, she carefully avoided any further contact with the barbed wire and gingerly emerged from underneath the bushes. No reaction elsewhere – there was no sight nor sound of any other animal. She hopped a little further downslope and then risked putting some weight on the damaged forefoot. Ouch! It hurt, though it was not unbearable. Then, standing a little crookedly, Madeleine held her breath and looked about her. It was OK: she was alone.

Limping slowly, she set off towards the fence. Madeleine

stopped every now and again and twisted her head round to see if she could see any movement above her, but still there was no sign of any dogs, nor of her partner. She kept going. Her first priority was to get to the fence as quickly as she could. Disabled and out in the open, she was a very vulnerable target and her heart was pounding nervously all the way. But no matter how much she fretted anxiously over her danger, she could not stop her thoughts from turning time and time again back to this wonderful, shadowy grey creature she had just come to know. How much did she *really* know about him? Not much! Who was he? Where was he from and why was he here? And how come he just drifted in and out of the farm and over this mountainside as he pleased? He seemed to have no limits, restrictions, inhibitions; he did all these things that she had never thought possible, defying all laws of man, cat and beast. She was fascinated, captivated, bewitched by him.

At last she reached the fence. There was nothing for it now; she had to prepare herself for a very painful climb! Screwing up her courage, she leapt, clung on with all the fires of pain travelling up her foreleg, and then she pushed up once more, in order to reach the top, twist round and drop herself over the other side. Thump! She hit the ground with three legs and pitched over clumsily, trying to avoid putting her damaged paw underneath her.

She rose rather self-consciously from the farmyard floor, spitting out dust from her mouth, hoping no animal had seen her rather ungainly tumble. She was a proud, normally elegant young feline and she hated the idea of anyone she knew seeing her uncharacteristic sprawl.

No one was in sight. She grimaced wryly at her own reactions – despite all her new experiences and the new life she had begun to see over there in the woods, back in the world she was accustomed to she had immediately returned to her former mind-set: worried about what others would think, about how she appeared, about what image she presented to the world.

Mind you, there was something very important to worry about now – what Duke was going to do to her when she returned. She grimaced again. Maybe this time she was not about to be ripped apart by murderous killers, but whatever was coming was not going to be particularly nice. She limped across the yard with a sinking heart.

Duke was waiting for her at the foot of the ladder to the hayloft. Despite the gloom in the interior of the barn, she could see he was beside himself with fury at the sight of her: wild and totally out of control of himself. She did not stop; she did not look up; she did not care any more. Tired and in pain, she limped forward and accepted what was to come. She had no choice.

Duke raged and fumed and screamed at her. She heard nothing. Blows rained down on her head and body – she was bitten, scratched and pummelled, rolled over and hammered again. Still Duke continued swearing at her but she was deaf to it all. The fact that this female was dumb and reactionless to all his tirades seemed to drive Duke to even greater violence. Now he really began to hurt her. One or two clawing blows seemed to bite deep into her soul. At last Madeleine could not stop herself: she began to cry.

"Stop! Stop! You've hurt her enough! How much more are you going to hit her? You will do her a major injury in a minute!" Elizabeth, the eldest of the three females, called down from the hayloft above.

"I'll hit her and keep hitting her until I'm done," the tomcat growled back, breathing hard. "She'll never do this again! Never!" Bang – another blow smacked around her head. "Will you, eh? You'll never disobey me again, will you?"

Madeleine cried in pain. She could not speak.

"Answer me, you bitch! You won't disobey me, will you?" Duke said it with all the spite and venom at his command. He held her firmly with his front paws and raked her with powerful hind legs. He hated her independence and he was determined to break her spirit and wring this concession out of her at all costs. "WILL YOU?" he screamed at her.

Madeleine was trapped and it hurt right down to the depths of her being. She cried unreservedly; she cried from deep within her; she felt as if her life was being snuffed out. Finally, she gave in:

"No… no… never…" It was torn out of her.

Only then did Duke let go. She did not move. She lay crumpled in the straw, scratched and beaten at the foot of the ladder. She wanted to die. She *was* dead now, it seemed to her hallucinating mind: there was nothing more left in this life that could mean anything to her.

Panting with the exertion but gloatingly triumphant, the bullying tomcat swaggered off. He felt satisfied that not only would this one never cross him again but he had given a good lesson to all the others in the barn as well. The two other females and the five kittens had seen it all from above. They knew who was king.

When he had gone, Pippa and Elizabeth crept down the ladder, desperately worried. They reached their cousin and licked her poor body, whispering to her, trying to revive her. Madeleine moaned:

"Leave me alone. Let me die!"

"No! Come on, Madeleine, come back with us. You cannot just lie here and give up!" Pippa was weeping at all that she had seen, but Elizabeth was a more mature and sensible cat who knew what had to be done. She took control of the situation.

Wilson left the narrow rabbit path and climbed up. Bounding sure-footedly from block to block, he soon reached the top of the rock tower. From there he could see that where he stood was in fact only one feature in an outcrop which descended in a slanting line from the mountain's summit some distance above.

Something drew him in this direction. He did not know why, but he had to go on. It was as if something inside him was answering to a deeper calling. Up there – where the mountaintop stood dark and erect against the blue sky – he knew that was his destination, where he would find the Moonlight Cat.

He was meanwhile confident that, even if she had not yet reached the farm by now, Madeleine would no longer be troubled by the remaining hound. That poor animal would be in mourning for his fallen brother and would not return to patrol the slopes below for some time yet. Wilson could continue on his journey with his conscience untroubled.

It was a long way to go. It was also a barren and exposed terrain which no ordinary cat would ever contemplate crossing, being more appropriate for sheep and goats. The weather was not unwelcoming, however, and Wilson's short, thick fur was more than adequate to keep him warm as he climbed higher and higher.

At last, in the late afternoon of this long and eventful day, Wilson reached the summit. The rock towers here were broken and frost-shattered but they stood high and proud, jutting out majestically above the panorama all around. Wilson padded out along the final arête and then settled down to take in the view: his head to the wind, his back braced against the rock, a tiny grey shadow in a great immensity of space.

It was utterly awe-inspiring. There was a grandeur; a richness; a dazzling complexity of detail but simplicity of overall one-ness that was staggering in its impact. Wilson felt as if his eyes, his brain could never be big enough to assimilate it all. The World rolled away in every direction, yet each tiny dot on its surface was an entire world in itself! There, far below, he knew was the farm from where he had come. And *there* was the barn, the farmhouse and the glasshouses opposite – all in a tiny world of their own, so different yet no doubt so similar to all the other buildings and farmyards he could see. And right over there –

dark and smoggy yet glowing dully in its own light: a sprawling blanket of houses, concrete and glass – was that The City he knew, or another? He could not tell. That was only one corner of the huge canvas that was spread out all around him.

He felt so small.

He felt at peace: here at last was what the Moonlight Cat could see, had always seen – the beauty of it all.

"Gives you a different outlook on life, doesn't it!" It was a statement, more than a question.

Without having to look, Wilson knew the soft voice behind him belonged to old Fabio, the tortoiseshell cat.

"Yes... it does. You can sort of understand everything... yet understand nothing. Isn't that so!" Wilson replied in the same rhetorical manner.

One cat and a Shadow sat together in silent contemplation, both looking out on the world, sharing the same thoughts.

"You know, you can look at this for a lifetime and more; grapple with it; finally come to terms with it... and yet you *keep* on meeting others who, even if you brought them up here and showed them it all, they still could not see further than the tips of their own whiskers..."

Wilson snorted: "Aren't they all like that?"

"No, thankfully not. There are many who are seeking the true path – though it takes much time and even more tolerance to be able to recognise them."

"But there seem to be so many who will never understand... Is it so wrong to be intolerant?"

"Well no, not if that is truly your way... it's just that it is not His Way."

"Mmm..."

"Remember, when you are down there, surrounded and overwhelmed by detail, you have got to see it ALL – the wholeness... the beauty... as if you were here all the time. Only then can you see others with tolerance, with love."

"What if the detail that is overwhelming you comes in the form of violence? How can you love and tolerate that?"

"Violence is always and everywhere destructive. You must see that first of all. Then, when you *really* understand that, you will never initiate it nor reply with it yourself. You will, however, find a way to turn violence in on itself. You already know this, don't you? Isn't that what you did just a little while ago, below?"

"Mmmm…"

"When you leapt at that dog below, was it with hatred? With a desire to hurt him, to make him suffer? Or were you trying to turn him back? The instant that you took action, what were you *feeling*?"

"It… it wasn't hatred… I guess it was determination to stop him, somehow… I didn't want to *hurt* him…"

"*You* didn't hurt him. You gave him a mere scratch on the back. But he hurt himself, didn't he? He could not attack you and save himself at the same time – yet he instinctively chose to attack. It was the wrong Way… and it was his undoing. Violence directed at others always hurts the perpetrator in the end – in this case, more quickly, more dramatically than you could have foreseen.

"But you already know so much, Wilson. Unlike that poor hound, by your actions you show that you instinctively follow His Way. Look a little deeper. *Examine* your instincts. I have told you before – the path outside is followed first by looking inside. You have little further need to question me on these matters: question yourself. *Always* question. Seek the truth within yourself. The more you look, the deeper you go, the closer you will come to finding the Love that binds us all together. And isn't that exactly what you see reflected here, spread out all around us, from the tiptop of this mountain to the faraway horizons? The Way of The Moonlight Cat…"

The voice of old Fabio trailed away into silence. Wilson knew that, if he turned now, he would see those bright, shining eyes fading away into the evening mists.

He remained stock-still, thinking. There was so much to take in. Physically, emotionally, spiritually, Wilson suddenly realised how tired he was. Silently, still wrapped in his own thoughts, he walked back along the arête, dropped down out of the wind and curled up in a fissure of the rock to rest. He fell asleep in seconds.

Elizabeth would not leave her alone. With Pippa's help, she half-carried, half-cajoled Madeleine back up the ladder into the hayloft. There she settled her down as comfortably as possible, washed her wounds, fetched across a bowl of water for Madeleine to drink and tried her best to encourage and revive her spirits.

Madeleine lay motionless, unresponsive, dead at first to all her cousin's efforts on her behalf. She was back under the spell of Duke, her master. Her soul had been savaged, her spirit crushed. The spark of independence which had burned deep within her had been all but extinguished. She had agreed to Duke's supremacy, his right to decide her destiny. She was *his* female. How could she live again?

Pippa and the kittens retreated to the far end of the hayloft, silenced and fearful at the dreadful turn of events that they had witnessed. An air of gloom and pessimism would have enveloped the whole company, had it not been for Elizabeth. She was a very practical cat and busied about, refusing to accept the spread of defeatism that threatened to infect everyone. She sent Pippa across to the farmhouse to retrieve the food that still remained from their earlier meal. The kittens were enjoined to tidy up the hayloft – a tiresome and unrewarding task which, for the first time, they agreed to without a murmur of complaint. Although she did not want to, Madeleine was forced to eat something. Guessing her cousin would recover all the quicker if her body was given food, Elizabeth ignored Madeleine's weak attempts at refusal and insisted on having her way. Slowly, subtly, the atmosphere changed from one of silence and fear to one of noise and bustle and something like normality again.

Evening wore on into night. Outside, the mountain breathed out as darkness fell, giving up its warmth to the clear, cloudless skies. As the hours passed, a biting cold slowly spread across the summit, spilling over the cliffs to go rolling down the mountainside in slow waves. Inside the barn, Madeleine's exhaustion and despair at last gave way to a fitful kind of sleep. Meanwhile, the others in the hayloft burrowed into the straw to escape the cold, each one anxious to close their eyes and draw a veil over the distressing events of the day before.

The crescent moon rose brilliantly in the night sky above. Slowly, slowly it traced out a path across the heavens. In the dark, fresh, frosty air it seemed to throw a myriad of shadows over the farmyard. Imperceptibly at first but with growing urgency, it called out, whispering to all the creatures of the dusk to rise and greet the wonder of the night. As before, one of the kittens was roused by its influence. He crawled determinedly over his brother and sisters to reach the barn end where it overlooked the yard below.

"Ouch! Gerroff! Waddya doing?"

"I can't sleep... I gotta look outside."

"Oh bother you!... C'mon then."

Others followed. Soon all five kittens lined the edge of the hayloft: all restless, fidgety, awoken by the call of the clear, moonlit mountainscape beyond.

"Wow! It all looks so different in this light, doesn't it?"

"Yeah! Wouldn't you just love to explore it all...?"

"No. Not over the fence, thank you."

"Hey! Look! Isn't that one of the dogs on the hillside? What's he doing out at this time?"

"Look at him, crazy bonzo! Wandering around lost."

"Hey! Bonzo! Lost your way? Nothing to chase?"

"Sssh! Don't!"

"LOOK! Above there... coming down over those rocks... Isn't... isn't it..."

"The Moonlight Cat!"

"Is it... can it be again...?"

"Look at it... floating down... It's gotta be Him..."

"Will... will the dog see Him?"

"Look!"

The distant but distinct feline shadow seemed to hover directly in front of the dog. The kittens all waited, mesmerised, watching to see what would happen.

"The dog's not moving!"

"How can it? It's the Moonlight Cat! You can't touch *Him*!"

The Shadow floated away. The dog, petrified for an instant, returned to its idle roaming. The kittens were all beside themselves with excitement, making enough noise to awaken the whole barn.

"The Moonlight Cat! The Moonlight Cat!"

"He's coming *closer*! Look!"

On the other side of the fence, the Shadow was drifting over the grassy slopes, moving down towards the telegraph pole just in front of the barn. All of a sudden, effortlessly, He was there, poised atop the fence, moonbeams glinting off his fur, his eyes shining like tiny lamps. It was the Moonlight Cat!

"Aaaaw!" The smallest kitten mewed in fear and wonder and backed off a little. She bumped into the legs of her mother who had now come to join them.

"Mummy... it's Him! He's come here..."

Elizabeth nodded. "Well if nothing else will raise your aunt now, He will."

These words filtered somehow into the consciousness of her cousin. With an effort, Madeleine pushed herself up and tiptoed forward as if in a dream. At the threshold of the hayloft she hesitated, shivering like a ghost and she sought the assistance of her two cousins, one on either side. Half in hope, half in fear, she looked out over the top of the kittens… and found her gaze met by the Moonlight Cat across the yard below. Her head began to swim.

"It is… it is… Him," she cried softly and sank back down into the straw.

An angry hissing rose up to everyone's ears. It was Duke. He had reached the fence from across the yard and was now glaring at this magical intruder, but there was no awestruck welcome issuing from his throat. He was snarling with mounting aggression. The kittens stared in amazement.

"What's he doing? He's surely not going to…"

"He can't attack the Moonlight Cat!"

"I don't *believe* it!"

Eyes wide with incredulity, they watched Duke gather himself and make a leap for the fence. He did not make it clean to the top but he clung on with strong forelegs and scrabbled the rest of the way up with pure willpower. In response, the Moonlight Cat seemed to fly away noiselessly along the narrow knife-edge. He then stopped, turned and waited, shimmering in the dark.

"Look! He's showing Duke The Way!"

"Is he gonna follow? He can't… he'll lose his balance!"

"He'll never make it!"

But sheer hatred drove him on. Cautiously, clumsily, the big tabby tomcat slid along the fence top. From their lookout, the kittens could not hear anything but they seemed to understand that this animal was clawing the wooden paling in determination not to fall, nor to lose his quarry.

The Moonlight Cat rose again and walked a little further ahead to reach the telegraph pole. There he seemed to flow up and across to one of the heavy cables. He floated out and waited there, all four feet in perfect balance on the cable and then *he simply, impossibly, turned round.*

It was Duke now who stared, open mouthed, at this silhouette against the stars. He could not believe what he had just seen.

There was no way he could follow it. With a wobble he lost his balance and, hurrying to recover, he had to launch himself into the dark on the other side of the fence.

The kittens watched as first Duke disappeared and then, moving down from cable to fence, the Moonlight Cat also leapt away and out of sight on to the hillside.

Nobody moved. All eyes were glued to the slopes beyond, illuminated by the sparkling moon, all waiting to see what creature reappeared where.

A Shadow seemed to dance away, upslope, towards the west. A larger, darker cat chased after it.

"Is that Duke? What's he up to?"

"He's going over there. Can you see? He's... he's going towards that dog..."

"Oh... oh..."

There was a distant eruption of noise: barking, screeching, growling; the sound of bodies moving around. Whatever was going on seemed to continue for an age. Suddenly there was a piercing cry. The kittens were silent: it all sounded very ominous.

The moon had moved lower now, and darkness and shadow made it difficult to see with clarity what was happening. Only one animal was discernible. It was the dog, with his head down and his hindquarters slowly circling round. A snuffling and scrabbling were the only sounds that remained. Then there was nothing but silence. And darkness.

Madeleine awoke to bright sunlight streaming in upon her resting place. She raised her head. There was no one else around, the kittens and her two cousins had vanished.

She yawned, stretched, and pulled herself up into the day.

Had it all been a dream? She seemed to have been asleep for days and days, and her head was still fuzzy with a kaleidoscope of images which wheeled around in her brain.

Looking down at her body she saw scratches, scrapes and

clumps of fur missing but she no longer felt any pain. In fact she felt really great, in perfect condition. She shook her head. Perhaps *this* was a dream now – it certainly looked like it with a halo of sunshine bathing all around her.

She crossed over to the ladder and slowly, elegantly, with all her natural poise as before, she descended to the barn floor below. The big, wide doors were swung open as usual and she sauntered out of the relative gloom into the brilliant sunlight.

There was someone waiting for her. It was a cat. Lithe and sleek with short, smoky-grey fur. His eyes were shining with welcome.

"You're free," he said simply.

END

The philosopher brought the evening to a close:

"What do we consider are the greatest truths? And why do we believe what we believe? Is it intuition? Reason? Revelation? Are we taught it by our elders? Or do we come to it through experience? The answers can only come from within us and it is our individual respon-sibility to search them out. That is our journey!"

His audience applauded. Except one.

As the party dispersed and drifted away in ones and twos, David turned to Julia. "Money and possessions are only extrinsic rewards. Are they enough for you?"

"If I can get plenty, that'll do very well for the time being, thank you," she replied.

"You will excuse me, I hope," said David, "if I say that it is like chasing after superficialities with your nose to the ground, sniffing around, without raising yourself up to take a look at the view from the top of the mountain."

"I excuse you," said Julia. "Each to his own."

END

Liberalis is a Latin word which evokes ideas of freedom, liberality, generosity of spirit, dignity, honour, books, the liberal arts education tradition and the work of the Greek grammarian and storyteller Antonius Liberalis. We seek to combine all these interlinked aspects in the books we publish.

We bring classical ways of thinking and learning in touch with traditional storytelling and the latest thinking in terms of educational research and pedagogy in an approach that combines the best of the old with the best of the new.

As classical education publishers, our books are designed to appeal to readers across the globe who are interested in expanding their minds in the quest of knowledge. We cater for primary, secondary and higher education markets, homeschoolers, parents and members of the general public who have a love of ongoing learning.